GREAT AMERICAN GLASS
OF THE ROARING 20S AND DEPRESSION ERA

1998–1999 Value Guide

prepared by Bill Crowl and Berry Wiggins
(edited by James Measell)

Editor's note: Bill Crowl and Berry Wiggins have been buying and selling glassware made in the 1920s and the Depression Era for many years. Bill began collecting World's Fair memorabilia and coins in the early 1960s and soon branched out into Stretch glass and Carnival glass as well. Berry published *Stretch in Color* in the early 1970s, and he has collected glassware from the 1920s and Depression Era for several decades.

The values of collectible glassware may vary in regions of the country, but the **Three C's** (color, condition and collectibility) are always vital. The prices given here reflect items in mint condition. For decorated articles, the prices given are for the decoration as shown in the color pages of this book. Neither the authors nor the publisher can be held liable for any losses incurred when using this guide as the basis for any transaction.

		Fig.	Value	Fig.	Value	Fig.	Value	Fig.	Value
front cover		1	$ 45.00	21	$ 42.00	41	$ 43.00	60	$ 95.00 set
A	$ 250.00	2	25.00	22	45.00	42	130.00	61	160.00
B	9.00	3	55.00	23	85.00	43	95.00 pr	62	85.00
C	60.00	4	85.00	24	43.00	44	70.00	63	90.00
D	52.00	5	65.00	25	45.00	45	52.00	64	95.00
E	65.00	6	45.00	26	55.00	46	85.00	65	45.00
F	60.00	7	95.00	27	85.00	47	82.00 pr	66	90.00
G	85.00 set	8	75.00	28	55.00	48	75.00	67	35.00
		9	85.00	29	55.00	49	90.00	68	60.00
back cover		10	42.00	30	35.00	50	75.00	69	75.00
H	95.00	11	65.00	31	135.00	51	45.00	70	125.00
I	135.00	12	85.00	32	55.00	52	38.00	71	45.00
J	25.00	13	55.00	33	35.00	53	65.00 pr	72	45.00
K	20.00	14	65.00	34	37.00	54	30.00	73	115.00
L	85.00	15	65.00	35	45.00 set	55	62.00	74	90.00 pr
M	60.00	16	55.00	36	85.00	55A	52.00	75	85.00
N	85.00	17	60.00	37	45.00 set	56	40.00	76	95.00 pr
O	50.00	18	20.00	38	38.00	57	38.00	77	95.00
		19	63.00	39	42.00	58	65.00 pr	78	75.00
		20	95.00	40	75.00	59	33.00	79	80.00

Fig.	Value	Fig.	Value	Fig.	Value	Fig.	Value	Fig.	Value
80	$ 45.00	124	$ 37.00 set	169	$ 60.00 pr	214	$ 35.00	259	$175.00
81	95.00	125	45.00	170	65.00	215	25.00	260	30.00
82	45.00	126	60.00 pr	171	110.00 pr	216	85.00	261	48.00
83	65.00	127	50.00	172	70.00	217	65.00	262	28.00
84	25.00	128	45.00	173	50.00	218	25.00	263	75.00
85	20.00	129	48.00	174	50.00	219	95.00	264	42.00
86	45.00	130	45.00	175	38.00	220	35.00	265	65.00
87	38.00	131	60.00 pr	176	95.00	221	75.00	266	20.00
88	47.00	132	57.00	177	35.00	222	75.00 pr	267	20.00
89	38.00	133	35.00	178	30.00	223	38.00	268	35.00
90	45.00 pr	134	45.00	179	75.00	224	38.00	269	45.00
91	55.00	135	35.00	180	50.00	225	35.00	270	45.00
92	35.00	136	35.00	181	45.00	226	45.00	271	35.00
93	20.00	137	38.00	182	65.00	227	20.00	272	50.00
94	20.00	138	35.00	183	50.00	228	28.00	273	35.00
95	40.00	139	55.00	184	40.00	229	55.00	274	45.00
96	85.00 pr	140	30.00	185	27.00	230	75.00 set	275	35.00
97	48.00	141	125.00 pr	186	42.00	231	110.00 set	276	35.00
98	95.00	142	85.00	187	45.00	232	70.00 pr	277	35.00
99	42.00	143	45.00	188	35.00	233	40.00	278	35.00
100	55.00	144	35.00	189	35.00	234	70.00 pr	27	45.00
101	65.00	145	80.00 pr	190	45.00	235	50.00	280	65.00
102	30.00	146	55.00	191	35.00	236	35.00	281	50.00
103	30.00	147	80.00 pr	192	55.00	237	55.00	282	40.00
104	55.00	148	60.00	193	75.00 pr	238	50.00	283	40.00
105	45.00	149	37.00	194	60.00	239	35.00	284	40.00
106	35.00	150	55.00	195	65.00	240	38.00	285	45.00
107	45.00	151	35.00	196	950.00	241	48.00	286	45.00
108	55.00	152	35.00	197	40.00	242	38.00	287	45.00
109	45.00	153	25.00	198	70.00 pr	243	38.00	288	40.00
110	65.00 pr	154	25.00	199	60.00	244	35.00	289	30.00
110A	30.00	155	25.00	200	35.00	245	45.00	290	40.00
111	75.00	156	55.00	201	35.00	246	55.00	291	50.00
112	40.00	157	75.00	202	15.00	247	45.00	292	30.00
113	45.00	158	85.00	203	35.00	248	60.00 set	293	75.00
114	70.00	159	25.00	204	25.00 set	249	350.00 set	294	40.00
115	45.00	160	25.00	205	25.00	250	100.00 set	295	65.00
116	50.00	161	45.00	206	35.00	251	15.00	296	5.00
117	45.00 pr	162	75.00 pr	207	48.00	252	35.00	297	10.00
118	50.00	163	85.00	208	48.00 set	253	38.00	298	7.00
119	45.00 pr	164	45.00	209	25.00	254	20.00	299	8.00
120	40.00	165	48.00	210	50.00	255	75.00	300	35.00
121	40.00	166	53.00	211	52.00	256	95.00	301	7.00
122	45.00	167	48.00	212	25.00	257	20.00	302	8.00
123	35.00	168	45.00	213	25.00	258	30.00	303	7.00

Fig.	Value	Fig.	Value	Fig.	Value	Fig.	Value	Fig.	Value
304	$ 35.00	349	$ 15.00	394	$ 75.00	439	$115.00	484	$ 60.00
305	10.00	350	45.00	395	30.00	440	45.00	485	90.00 pr
306	12.00	351	35.00	396	25.00	441	35.00	486	80.00
307	15.00	352	40.00	397	35.00	442	40.00	487	40.00
308	110.00	353	45.00	398	37.00	443	45.00	488	45.00
309	50.00	354	20.00	399	35.00	444	50.00	489	45.00
310	250.00	355	45.00	400	60.00	445	60.00	490	55.00
311	250.00	356	47.00	401	45.00	446	40.00	491	15.00
312	350.00	357	300.00	402	60.00	447	65.00	492	55.00
313	15.00	358	35.00	403	40.00	448	60.00	493	50.00
314	20.00	359	250.00	404	30.00	449	50.00	494	65.00
315	25.00	360	85.00	405	55.00	450	45.00	495	90.00
316	25.00	361	25.00	406	20.00	451	40.00	496	50.00
317	30.00	362	175.00	407	45.00	452	30.00	497	40.00
318	225.00	363	35.00	408	60.00 pr	453	35.00	498	45.00
319	20.00	364	30.00	409	45.00	454	65.00	499	45.00
320	20.00	365	40.00	410	35.00	455	85.00	500	42.00
321	80.00	366	40.00	411	18.00	456	70.00	501	45.00
322	110.00	367	85.00 pr	412	5.00	457	22.00	502	37.00
323	85.00	368	50.00	413	5.00	458	15.00	503	50.00
324	120.00	369	60.00	414	5.00	459	10.00	504	45.00
325	125.00	370	55.00	415	5.00	460	75.00	505	25.00
326	45.00	371	20.00	416	10.00	461	34.00	506	45.00
327	40.00	372	65.00	417	10.00 set	462	30.00	507	55.00
328	40.00	373	45.00	418	12.00	463	35.00	508	38.00
329	175.00 pr	374	45.00	419	11.00	464	30.00	509	250.00
330	150.00	375	60.00	420	23.00	465	25.00	510	325.00
331	85.00	376	45.00	421	35.00	466	10.00	511	50.00
332	325.00	377	40.00	422	40.00	467	37.00	512	35.00
333	125.00	378	50.00 pr	423	32.00	468	35.00	513	40.00
334	85.00	379	70.00	424	32.00	469	5.00 ea	514	40.00
335	125.00	380	45.00	425	7.00	470	50.00	515	30.00
336	65.00	381	47.00	426	8.00	471	45.00	516	35.00
337	115.00	382	45.00	427	7.00	472	30.00	517	40.00
338	145.00 pr	383	70.00	428	7.00	473	42.00	518	30.00
339	65.00	384	70.00	429	85.00	474	40.00	519	30.00
340	40.00	385	40.00	430	85.00	475	60.00	520	30.00
341	135.00 pr	386	45.00	431	35.00	476	55.00	521	35.00
342	45.00	387	30.00	432	32.00	477	40.00	522	30.00
343	65.00	388	30.00	433	35.00	478	75.00	523	30.00
344	40.00	389	30.00	434	85.00	479	125.00	524	30.00
345	37.00	390	32.00	435	32.00	480	75.00	525	20.00
346	42.00	391	70.00 pr	436	65.00	481	40.00	526	25.00
347	75.00	392	45.00	437	45.00	482	45.00	527	65.00 pr
348	20.00	393	50.00	438	55.00	483	75.00	528	50.00

GEORGIAN TUMBLERS:

Look quickly at Figs. 257-258, 316, 319-320, and 878 in this book. These are all 9 oz. Georgian pattern tumblers, and, at first glance, they all look pretty much alike! How can you tell which factory made which tumbler? The capacity in ounces really varies, even though all are classified as 9 oz. tumblers by the manufacturers. So, filling them with water won't help! First, you need to learn how to determine the number and placement of mould joints on a Georgian tumbler. Second, you need to measure the key areas of the tumbler. Let's take it a step at a time.

Georgian tumblers were made in either two-part moulds or four-part moulds. Those from two-part moulds will have two "joint marks" visible on the outside near the base or bottom of the tumbler (these will be 180 degrees from each other or, if you prefer, on "opposite" sides of the tumbler). Those from four-part moulds will have four joint marks, one on each "quarter" of the tumbler as you turn it in your hand.

Now that you've determined the number of mould marks, here are some guidelines for the tumblers made by several manufacturers: Duncan-Miller made Georgian tumblers in both two-part and four-part moulds; Beaumont and Fenton used four-part moulds only, and Central and Paden City used two-part moulds only. Follow one of the joint marks up the side of the tumbler; if the joint mark follows the lines in the Georgian pattern, you've got a Georgian tumbler made in a hand glass plant. It could be a Duncan-Miller, Fenton or Paden City product (or from Beaumont or Central, two other firms which also made Georgian tumblers). If the joint mark goes straight up through the pattern, you've got a Georgian tumbler made by an automatic machine; it could have been made by any of several different plants, and there doesn't seem to be any foolproof way to separate these from one another.

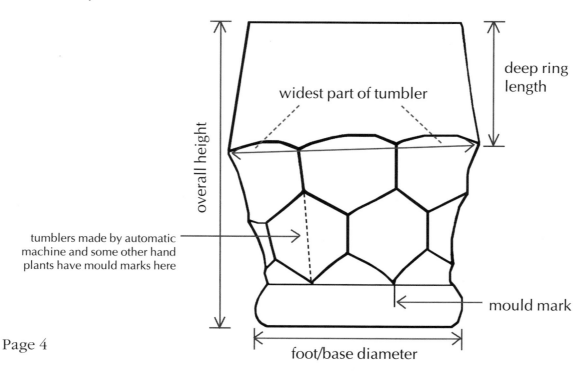

deep ring length

widest part of tumbler

overall height

tumblers made by automatic machine and some other hand plants have mould marks here

mould mark

foot/base diameter

WHO MADE WHAT?

Now that you know the number of joint marks (and that the joint follows the angles of the pattern), let's get ready to do some serious measuring! If you are dealing with several tumblers you might want to put stickers on each one (or a small piece of paper inside) to record your measurements. You'll need a caliper rule and a steel tape measure with a hook at the end (Berry Wiggins prefers a Stanley brand with 1/16 graduations). Brad Gougeon loaned him about 40 Georgian tumblers several years ago, and Berry perfected these steps by measuring these tumblers and talking with "Eddie" Ungar:

1. Turn the tumbler upside down and measure the diameter of the base or foot. Measure in three different places because the foot may not be perfectly round. Record your measurements to the closest sixteenth of an inch.

2. Measure the overall height of the tumbler. This will vary a bit within a given company, but it will help you separate the tall Paden City tumblers from the shorter ones made at Beaumont or Central. Record your measurements to the closest sixteenth of an inch.

3. Measure the length of the deep ring—from the top of the tumbler to the tip of one of the long points on the pattern. Hook your tape on the top rim of the tumbler and pull it snug, making sure the tape is straight. Measure five or six points and use the greatest measurement. Record your measurement to the closest sixteenth of an inch.

4. Use the caliper rule to measure the widest part of the tumbler, just where the Georgian pattern begins. You might find it helpful to slide the caliper rule down the sides of the tumbler to the widest point, after which it will "drop off" the tumbler. Measure in two or three different places. Record your measurements to the closest sixteenth of an inch.

Now, compare your Georgian tumbler with the chart below. Check carefully to be sure your tumbler fits all the characteristics. Who made your tumbler? Watch for more information about Georgian tumblers in the next book.

MANUFACTURER	NO. OF JOINTS	FOOT/ BASE DIA.	OVERALL HEIGHT	DEEP RING LENGTH	WIDEST PART OF TUMBLER
Beaumont	4	$2^{12}/_{16}$	$3^{12}/_{16}$-$^{15}/_{16}$	$1^{14}/_{16}$	$3^{5}/_{16}$
Central	2	$2^{10}/_{16}$-$^{13}/_{16}$	$3^{13}/_{16}$-4	$1^{14}/_{16}$-$^{15}/_{16}$	$3^{4}/_{16}$-$^{5}/_{16}$
Duncan-Miller	4	$2^{10}/_{16}$-$^{12}/_{16}$	$3^{15}/_{16}$	$1^{15}/_{16}$	$3^{4}/_{16}$-$^{5}/_{16}$
Duncan-Miller	2	$2^{13}/_{16}$	$3^{15}/_{16}$	2	$3^{6}/_{16}$
Fenton	4	$2^{10}/_{16}$-$^{13}/_{16}$	$3^{15}/_{16}$-4	$1^{15}/_{16}$-2	$3^{5}/_{16}$-$^{6}/_{16}$
Paden City	2	$2^{12}/_{16}$	$4^{2}/_{16}$	2	$3^{4}/_{16}$

Fig.	Value	Fig.	Value	Fig.	Value	Fig.	Value	Fig.	Value
529	$ 85.00 pr	574	$ 30.00	619	$ 50.00	664	$ 50.00 pr	705	$ 75.00
530	75.00	575	30.00	620	175.00	665	45.00	706	45.00
531	75.00 pr	576	27.00	621	25.00	666	80.00 pr	707	40.00
532	85.00	577	30.00	622	25.00	667	30.00	708	45.00
533	65.00 pr	578	85.00	623	10.00	668	55.00	709	40.00
534	50.00	579	15.00	624	15.00	669	40.00	710	65.00
535	35.00	580	30.00	625	35.00	670	35.00	711	45.00
536	55.00 pr	581	35.00	626	150.00	671	50.00	712	12.00 ea
537	45.00	582	30.00	627	20.00	672	35.00 pr	713	32.00
538	50.00	583	32.00	628	20.00	673	23.00	714	40.00
539	42.00	584	15.00	629	17.00 set	674	27.00	715	35.00
540	35.00	585	22.00	630	10.00	675	22.00	716	27.00
541	35.00	586	32.00	631	20.00	676	20.00	717	25.00
542	45.00	587	22.00	632	10.00	677	38.00	718	18.00 set
543	45.00	588	35.00	633	10.00	678	22.00	719	28.00
544	25.00	589	20.00	634	8.00	679	25.00	720	45.00
545	40.00	590	35.00	635	45.00	680	30.00	721	35.00
546	22.00	591	27.00	636	30.00	681	48.00	722	40.00
547	45.00	592	18.00	637	20.00	682	48.00	723	35.00
548	40.00	593	30.00	638	75.00	683	27.00	724	40.00
549	37.00	594	35.00	639	15.00	684	35.00	725	45.00
550	42.00	595	32.00	640	110.00	685	35.00 pr	726	45.00
551	4.00 ea	596	50.00	641	15.00	686	40.00	727	50.00
552	27.00	597	35.00 pr	642	100.00	687	42.00	728	40.00
553	30.00 pr	598	35.00 pr	643	110.00	688	35.00	729	47.00
554	32.00	599	45.00	644	20.00	689	12.00	730	45.00
555	40.00	600	45.00	645	20.00	690	21.00	731	37.00
556	25.00 pr	601	32.00	646	30.00	691	42.00	732	48.00
557	20.00	602	35.00	647	50.00	692	25.00	733	50.00
558	45.00	603	35.00	648	35.00	693	48.00	734	35.00
559	15.00	604	30.00	649	45.00	694	35.00	735	48.00
560	16.00	605	25.00	650	35.00	695	40.00	736	50.00
561	16.00	606	45.00	651	45.00	696	20.00	737	45.00
562	18.00	607	55.00 pr	652	25.00	697	20.00	738	37.00
563	18.00	608	32.00	653	25.00	698	32.00	739	48.00
564	15.00	609	28.00	654	45.00	699	12.00	740	42.00
565	25.00 pr	610	45.00	655	45.00	700	25.00	741	50.00
566	15.00	611	47.00	656	27.00			742	30.00
567	12.00	612	35.00	657	30.00	**Note: Figs. 701, 703**		743	20.00
568	25.00 pr	613	65.00	658	20.00	**and 705–711 have**		744	70.00
569	28.00	614	65.00	659	150.00	**an iridescent finish.**		745	30.00
570	35.00	615	65.00	660	20.00			746	20.00
571	22.00	616	110.00	661	15.00	701	65.00	747	32.00
572	10.00	617	20.00	662	30.00	702	37.00	748	30.00
573	25.00	618	15.00	663	35.00	703	75.00	749	38.00
						704	38.00 pr		

Fig.	Value	Fig.	Value	Fig.	Value	Fig.	Value	Fig.	Value
750	$ 30.00	795	$ 30.00	840	$ 35.00	885	$ 32.00	930	$ 20.00
751	50.00	796	95.00	841	45.00	886	25.00	931	35.00
752	32.00	797	45.00	842	40.00	887	25.00	932	65.00
753	35.00	798	85.00 set	843	60.00	888	48.00	933	55.00
754	35.00	799	30.00 set	844	75.00	889	48.00	934	32.00
755	45.00	800	40.00	845	70.00	890	7.00	935	47.00
756	50.00	801	75.00 set	846	30.00	891	28.00	936	47.00
757	40.00	802	60.00 set	847	45.00	892	45.00	937	38.00
758	45.00	803	75.00 set	848	45.00	893	27.00	938	62.00
759	27.00	804	25.00	849	35.00	894	25.00	939	70.00
760	60.00	805	65.00	850	35.00	895	125.00	940	48.00
761	45.00	806	90.00	851	55.00	896	25.00	941	42.00
762	15.00	807	125.00	852	37.00	897	28.00	942	40.00
763	15.00	808	35.00	853	90.00	898	35.00	943	45.00
764	25.00	809	150.00	854	30.00	899	52.00	944	43.00
765	30.00	810	145.00 pr	855	45.00	900	40.00	945	45.00
766	100.00	811	90.00	856	45.00	901	37.00	946	48.00
767	45.00	812	65.00	857	45.00	902	42.00	947	175.00 set
768	38.00	813	50.00	858	47.00	903	40.00	948	40.00
769	47.00	814	65.00	859	25.00	904	53.00	949	85.00 pr
770	45.00	815	110.00	860	25.00	905	27.00	950	75.00 pr
771	35.00	816	125.00	861	30.00	906	60.00	951	95.00 pr
772	45.00	817	35.00	862	20.00	907	45.00	952	45.00
773	42.00	818	95.00	863	60.00 pr	908	32.00	953	25.00
774	45.00	819	85.00	864	40.00	909	45.00	954	45.00
775	75.00	820	80.00	865	25.00	910	35.00	955	45.00
776	40.00	821	45.00	866	25.00	911	40.00	956	65.00
777	65.00	822	70.00 pr	867	40.00	912	85.00 pr	957	28.00
778	45.00	823	90.00	868	15.00	913	40.00	958	42.00
779	35.00	824	45.00	869	42.00	914	45.00	959	45.00
780	65.00	825	95.00 pr	870	60.00	915	40.00		(satin finish)
781	50.00	826	70.00	871	28.00	916	25.00	960	40.00
782	35.00	827	65.00	872	50.00	917	30.00	961	115.00 pr
783	40.00	828	45.00	873	35.00	918	40.00		(satin finish)
784	15.00	829	60.00	874	55.00	919	45.00	962	52.00
785	42.00	830	20.00	875	48.00	920	35.00	963	150.00 pr
786	50.00	831	85.00	876	45.00	921	55.00	964	55.00
787	45.00	832	45.00	877	37.00	922	40.00	965	65.00
788	85.00	833	125.00 pr	878	24.00	923	50.00	966	65.00
789	200.00	834	125.00	879	30.00	924	48.00	967	175.00
790	35.00	835	250.00	880	43.00	925	38.00	968	75.00
791	40.00	836	95.00	881	35.00	926	75.00	969	85.00
792	25.00	837	45.00	882	37.00	927	42.00	970	250.00
793	30.00 set	838	45.00	883	55.00	928	65.00	971	80.00
794	110.00 pr	839	50.00	884	25.00	929	35.00	972	110.00

Fig.	Value	Fig.	Value	Fig.	Value	Fig.	Value	Fig.	Value
973	$115.00	1002	$95.00	1030	$85.00	1059	$30.00	1088	$60.00
974	85.00	1003	20.00	1031	50.00	1060	25.00	1089	15.00
975	85.00	1004	25.00	1032	85.00	1061	32.00	1090	75.00
976	105.00	1005	25.00	1033	80.00 pr	1062	38.00	1091	15.00
977	80.00	1006	20.00	1034	70.00	1063	100.00	1092	70.00
978	85.00	1007	80.00 pr	1035	80.00 pr	1064	125.00	1093	15.00
979	45.00 pr	1008	65.00	1036	70.00	1065	35.00	1094	70.00
980	95.00 pr	1009	85.00 pr	1037	75.00	1066	55.00	1095	15.00
981	90.00	1009A	80.00	1038	40.00	1067	55.00	1096	70.00
982	110.00	1010	45.00	1039	37.00	1068	38.00	1097	15.00
983	85.00	1011	50.00	1040	35.00	1069	20.00	1098	70.00
984	95.00	1012	55.00	1041	40.00	1070	35.00	1099	15.00
985	85.00	1013	25.00	1042	35.00	1071	25.00	1100	65.00
986	95.00	1014	45.00	1043	32.00	1072	25.00	1101	20.00
987	114.00	1015	35.00	1044	35.00	1073	40.00	1102	20.00
988	175.00	1016	40.00	1045	25.00	1074	37.00	1103	65.00
989	55.00 pr	1017	45.00	1046	38.00	1075	15.00	1104	12.00 ea
990	95.00	1018	28.00	1047	50.00	1076	85.00	1105	50.00
991	90.00	1019	35.00	1048	30.00	1077	15.00	1106	100.00
992	125.00	1020	100.00 pr	1049	75.00	1078	75.00	1107	15.00
993	80.00	1021	50.00	1050	65.00	1079	12.00	1108	12.00
994	130.00 pr	1022	52.00	1051	60.00	1080	65.00	1109	60.00
995	110.00	1023	55.00	1052	35.00	1081	12.00	1110	95.00 set
996	90.00	1024	38.00	1053	60.00	1082	70.00	1111	37.00
997	65.00	1025	125.00	1054	50.00	1083	15.00	1112	35.00
998	75.00	1026	40.00	1055	45.00	1084	75.00	1113	55.00
999	95.00	1027	75.00 pr	1056	75.00	1085	120.00 set		
1000	120.00	1028	65.00	1057	45.00	1086	125.00 set		
1001	125.00	1029	125.00 pr	1058	35.00	1087	12.00		

GREAT AMERICAN GLASS

OF

THE ROARING 20S

&

DEPRESSION

ERA

JAMES MEASELL AND BERRY WIGGINS

TABLE OF CONTENTS

INTRODUCTION

This book is the first volume of a series designed to provide a comprehensive overview, in color, of American glass from the 1920s and 1930s. These two decades, dubbed the "Roaring 20s" and the "Depression Era" by scholars and collectors alike, were marked by remarkable developments and technical innovations in the American glass tableware industry.

From 1860-1885, the epicenter of the tableware industry was Pittsburgh, although there were significant plants along the East Coast as well as the Ohio Valley near Wheeling, West Virginia. The "Gas Boom" in Northwestern Ohio during the late 1880s spread to central Indiana during the 1890s and then to Illinois, Kansas, Missouri and Oklahoma in the first decade of the twentieth century. The number of glass plants—bottle, window and tableware—grew dramatically, as investors rushed to back many former Pittsburgh or Ohio Valley glassmen in their new ventures.

By 1910, the gas had played out in many areas and competition had taken its toll in others. The glass tableware industry shifted back toward the Ohio Valley, although improved railroad transportation made it possible to locate factories along virtually any main line. At this time, the major players in the glass tableware industry were located as follows: Indiana (Indiana and Jenkins); Ohio (Cambridge, Heisey, Imperial); Pennsylvania (Diamond, Duncan Miller, McKee, and Westmoreland); and West Virginia (Central, Fenton, Fostoria, and Northwood). The United States Glass Company, with its headquarters in Pittsburgh, controlled factories in several of these states, and Hazel-Atlas also had interests in various places.

For many readers, the factory names in the paragraph above will be familiar ones. Yet, there were many others—such as Beaumont, Co-Operative Flint, Davies, Economy, Hocking, Jeannette, Lancaster, Liberty, New Martinsville, Paden City, Smith, and Vineland Flint—whose days were to come or whose prominence had not yet been realized. This book is, in a sense, the story of the lesser lights as well as the better-knowns. On the next several pages of this introduction, you will find facsimiles of original catalog pages and advertisements for glassware from the Roaring '20s and the Depression Era. Take the time and make the effort to study the shapes carefully. Peruse the descriptions of colors, and note the suggestions for the ways in which the pieces were intended to be used. Read "between the lines" and gain a sense of understanding the history of this period.

The times from 1908 to about 1915 had been dominated by the production of pattern glass sets and the manufacture of the iridescent glassware called "Carnival glass" today. Several major plants (Dugan [later Diamond], Imperial and Northwood) played important roles, and the short-lived Millersburg Glass Company had been active. To an extent, iridescent ware had established the new, relatively small Fenton factory. Although production of iridescent ware continued in the 1920s and 1930s, it had a smaller niche in the scheme of things in the American glass tableware industry.

Pattern glass sets slowly gave way to new styles of glassware in the 1920s. Those plants which had theretofore introduced two to four new pattern lines per year (each containing dozens of different items) began to produce utilitarian sets which contained multiples of the same item. In short, the "luncheon set," with its plates, cups and saucers, was born!

The July 26, 1928, issue of *Pottery, Glass and Brass Salesman* had this description of the various sets available: "There is the twelve piece bridge set, consisting of four each cups and saucers and four 8¹/₄ inch salad plates. There is a fifteen piece hostess set, the composition here being the same as in the bridge set, with the addition of sugar and creamer and a 14-inch platter. Then there is a twenty-one piece luncheon set made up of six each cups and saucers, six 8¹/₄ inch plates , a sugar and creamer and a 14-inch platter. The twenty-seven piece luncheon set is of the same combination, save that it supplies service for eight instead of six."

In some factory's sets, a sandwich tray with center handle took the place of the platter. Indeed, the sandwich tray—like the various candy jars and console sets shown in this book—is a glassware product that was originated and became popular in the 1920s and held its popularity throughout the Depression Era.

At first glance, all sandwich trays might seem to look much alike. But look more closely. As you view the color pages later in this book, notice the shapes of the handles on the various sandwich trays made by different factories. You'll see a "stirrup" as well as

(Text continued on page 10)

GLASSWARE FOR

Rose Pink New Optic Shape 29¢ EACH

Rose Pink Stem Ware 32¢ EACH

Graceful Water Set
Green or Rose Pink
A better quality water Set with graceful, highly polished optic pitcher and six light blown, optic tumblers of unusual design. Furnished in either of two dainty colors, Light Green or Rose Pink. Novelty colored glassware will add much to the brightness of your home and you will be unusually well pleased with this high grade set. Ship. weight, 8 lbs. State color wanted.
5C103A $1.89

Fine Stemware
Sold Only in Sets of 6
Fine light blown glassware, the kind that rings musically when you tap it. Graceful optic shape. New dainty rose pink color. High class yet not high priced. Sold in sets of six only.
5C184A Goblets. Set of 6. Ship. wt. 4 lbs. $1.74
5C185A Tall Sherbets. Set of 6. Ship. wt., 3½ lbs. $1.74
5C186A Low Sherbets. Set of 6. Ship. wt., 3½ lbs. $1.74

Floral hand cut design on graceful optic stemware. Tumbler to match. Crystal white or delicate Rose Pink. Light blown glassware of high quality. Sold only in sets of six.
		White	Pink
5C116A Tumblers. Set of 6. Ship. wt., 3 lbs.		$0.98	$1.35
5C118A Goblets. Set of 6. Ship. wt., 4 lbs.		1.85	2.10
5C119A Tall Sherbets. Set of 6. Ship. wt., 3½ lbs.		1.85	2.10
5C120A Low Sherbets. Set of 6. Ship. wt., 3 lbs.		1.85	2.10
5C140A Footed Creamer and Sugar bowl set in highly polished pressed glass. Hand cut Daisy design. Ship. wt., 3 lbs.		55c	

Fine Stemware
Sold Only in Sets of 6
Fine quality lead blown glassware. Novelty optic design, with new style needle etched decoration. Dainty rose pink color. Exceptionally low price for such high quality. Sold in sets of six only.
5C269A Goblets. Set of 6. Ship. wt., 4 lbs. $1.92
5C270A Tall Sherbets. Set of 6. Ship. wt., 3½ lbs. $1.92
5C271A Fruit Cocktails. Set of 6. Ship. wt., 3½ lbs. $1.92

7-Piece Water Set
Star Cut Design
A quality set of light blown glass consisting of tankard shaped pitcher and six flared glasses. Star design is hand cut and perfect. Cutware can be bought for less money but it is inferior in grade. We believe you want the best when you order cut glass so that is what we offer. Ship. wt., 8 lbs.
5C114A $1.49

Amber or Green
5C257A Console set in choice of Green or Amber color, consisting of 10-inch footed fruit or flower bowl and two tall candlesticks. A decorative set for buffet, serving or dining table. A remarkably pretty set for so low a price. Ship. wt., 8 lbs. State color wanted. Price. **$1.19**

15 Pc. Glass Party Set **$5.69**

New Octagon Shape—Green or Rose Pink
Glass Party Service, for four people, in the charming new octagon shape, choice of two colors, Green or Rose Pink. Set consists of 4 tea plates, 4 tea cups, 4 saucers, footed Cream Pitcher and Sugar bowl and handled Sandwich tray. The glass is highest quality pressed ware, each piece carefully moulded and highly polished. Your party luncheon or supper, served at card tables on this dainty ware, will be most appealing. Equally dainty and attractive for service on any occasion. Sold in sets only. Ship. wt., 25 lbs.
5C275A 15-Piece Set in Green $5.69
5C276A 15-Piece Set in Rose Pink $5.75

Colonial Console Set
5C130A An unusually attractive console set in the new Pale Green shade. Consists of 10½-inch flaring fin flower fruit bowl and two beautifully designed colonial low candlesticks. Makes an especially welcome gift. Ornamental for buffet or table. Our price of 98c is only about half of what many stores ask for this set. Ship. wt., about 5 lbs. Price. 98c

5C142A 7-piece Berry Set in green dull finish glass with ribbed bottom and rim in attractive machine cut design. Set consists of 8-inch berry bowl and six 4½-inch fruit dishes. Positively one of the biggest values you will find anywhere. Ship. wt., 6 lbs. 85c

5C136A Berry set in amber glass with golden iridescent luster. Especially attractive colonial design with fluted sides and plain edge. Set consists of 8-inch Berry Bowl and six 4½-inch fruit dishes. Ship. wt., about 6 lbs. Price. 67c

5C263A 9½-inch Flower Bowl, rose pink glass, with porcelain statuette flower holder. A very attractive set for centerpiece. Ship. wt., 5 lbs. Per set. $1.39

5C264 Measuring Cup with Lemon Squeezer, in Green Glass decorated with hand painted design. Squeezer fitted into cup or removed from cup in one turn. Ship. wt., 3 lbs. Each. 59c

Beautiful Opaque Glass, poppy design Flower Vase. Two colors, dull rose pink or dull black. Two sizes, 5 and 8 inches high. Useful for displaying flowers and decorative when not in use. Ship. wts.: 3½ and 6 lbs.
5C265A 5-inch size $0.59
5C266A 8-inch size 1.19

Cream and Sugar Set
5C101A Cream Pitcher and Sugar Bowl Set in new Pale Green shade pressed glass, decorated with dainty floral design. A very attractive set at a very low price. Ship. wt., about 2 lbs. Price. 49c

5C106A 12-piece Footed Sherbet and Plate Set in amber colored glass with golden iridescent luster. Used for serving sherbet, ice cream, pudding or berries. Set consists of six footed glasses and six plates. Ship. wt., about 6 lbs. Price. 98c

8 Pc. Matched Cut Glass Set **$5.69**

PIECES SOLD SEPARATELY

Beautiful 8-piece set, in Green or Rose Pink colors, consists of Handled Sandwich Tray, Footed Fruit or Flower Bowl, Footed Cake Salver, Cream Pitcher, Sugar Bowl and Mayonnaise Set of three pieces; footed bowl, ladle and plate. Made of high grade pressed glass, highly polished and hand cut in a particularly attractive new design. All pieces in this set are useful and desirable which has prompted us to offer it complete at a special price. You can also buy any piece singly if you wish.

5C284A 8-Piece Set. Wt., 25 lbs. $5.69
5C285 3-Piece Mayonnaise Set. Wt., 6 lbs. 1.19
5C286 Sandwich Tray. Wt., 5 lbs. 1.19
5C287 Footed Bowl. Wt., 5 lbs. 1.19
5C288 Footed Cake Salver. Wt., 5 lbs. 1.19
5C289 Creamer or Sugar Bowl. Wt., 5 lbs. 1.19

Amber Luster Water Set
5C113A A popular colonial design water set in amber colored glass with golden iridescent luster. Set consists of 3½-pint pitcher of attractive pattern and six 8-ounce tumblers. Such a set would cost much more at retail than our special low price of 98c. This is one of the biggest bargains we offer. Ship. wt., about 10 lbs. Price. 98c

7-Piece Water Set
Crystal or Green
Attractive new, pear optic design, light blown glassware, 7 piece water set. Choice of two colors, Crystal (clear) or the new Springtime Green. Set consists of tankard shaped pitcher and six 8-ounce tumblers. Note how low our price is for such a set in high class, light blown glassware. You will surely be greatly pleased if you select it. Ship. wt., about 5 lbs.
5C281A Crystal $0.95
5C282A Green 1.09

6

BEAUTY and UTILITY

Colonial Water Set
Special value 7-piece Colonial Water Set in fire polished, beautifully finished pressed glass. Set consists of handsome three pint pitcher and six 8-ounce tumblers. Heavy enough to be serviceable yet pleasing in design and appearance. Note our special low price. Ship. wt. 7 lbs.
5C102A   Per set 59c

Cake Salver

9-inch pressed glass Footed Cake Salver, fire polished and beautiful in design. Artistically figured. Shallow scalloped rim. Priced very low and one of our most popular sellers. Ship. wt., about 3½ lbs.
5C110A Each............ 39c

Richly Decorated Fruit Bowl
Fruit Bowl decorated in Rose design, tinted in natural colors on under side of glass. Artistic and beautiful. A handsome piece for side board or dining table. Diameter, 8 inches. Ship. wt., about 3 lbs.
5C268A 39c

Large 8-inch Flower Vase

Made of glass with rough surface having bird and grape vine design embossed to stand out in relief. Background in black with bird and vine decorated in bright colors. Striking, beautiful and up-to-date. 8 inches high. Wide mouth. Ship. wt., 2 lbs.
5C258A 29c

Baking Dish Set

BAKING DISH SET in the famous Rockingham finish earthenware, made up of four desirable sizes, one each. 5½, 6½, 7½ and 8½ inches. Made purposely to insure quick baking and a large area of delicious crust. Ship. wt., about 5 lbs.
5C191 Baking Set... 95c

Glass Baking Dish Set

Glass baking dishes give most satisfactory results for general pie or pie baking. Guaranteed to withstand intense heat. Set consists of three 8-inch dishes. Ship. wt., 4 lbs.
5C111A Set of 3 dishes........ 55c

Glassware Items Illustrated Here—Listed in Numerical Order Below
5C104A Light blown Tumbler with pretty, sand blast, wreath and basket design. Ship. wt., per doz., about 4 lbs. Per ½ dozen............ 38c Per dozen............ 75c
5C115A Combination Measuring Cup and Lemon Reamer. A handy utensil. Reamer locks in cup with one turn and is as easily removed. 1 Pint Squat Cup is marked for measure in pints, cups and ounces. Ship. wt., about 3 lbs. Price............ 39c
5C121A 6-piece Table Set with artistic cut design in pressed glass consisting of 2-piece Sugar, Creamer, 2-piece Butter Dish and Spoonholder. Ship. wt., 5 lbs. 69c
5C124A Footed Sherbet Glasses of fire polished crystal glass. Height, 3¾ inches. Ship. wt., per doz., about 4 lbs. Per ½ dozen............ 47c Per dozen............ 90c
5C126 Salt and Pepper Shaker Sets. Colonial design. Aluminum dome top. Ship. wt., about 1 lb. Per pair............ 11c
5C128 Vinegar or Oil Bottle of clear pressed glass. Colonial design. Height, 7 inches. Ship. wt., about 1½ lbs. Price............ 23c
5C145A Jelly Glass with Tin Cover. One half pint capacity. Sold in dozen lots only. Ship. wt., 4 lbs. per dozen. Price............ 44c
5C154A Optic Blown Tumbler plain and neat in design. A popular style. Ship. wt., per dozen, about 6 lbs. Per ½ dozen............ 20c Per dozen............ 39c
5C188A 6-piece Colonial Table Set, of heavy fire polished crystal glass, consisting of 2-piece sugar bowl, cream pitcher, 2-piece butter dish and spoonholder. Ship. wt., about 6 lbs. Price............ 89c

11 Piece Glassware Set
$2.29 CRYSTAL GLASS $2.95 GREEN GLASS

Any Piece Sold Separately
This 11-piece set containing useful glassware pieces, is of Crystal or Green, highly polished pressed glass, in a lace design that has the appearance of hand cutting. You can buy any piece singly if you wish. Set consists of, 5-inch Mayonnaise Bowl and Ladle, 10½-inch Serving Plate, 10½-inch Footed Salad or Fruit Bowl, 11-inch Handled Sandwich Tray and Set of six 8-inch Salad Plates.

Green or Crystal

Number	Article	Wt., Lbs.	Crystal	Green
5C160A	11-piece set..	23	$2.29	$2.95
5C152A	Sandwich Tray	6	.49	.61
5C153A	Mayonnaise Set	4	.31	.41
5C192A	10-inch Plate	4	.31	.41
5C193A	10-inch Bowl..	7	.41	.57
5C194A	Set of 6, 8-in. Plates. ..	5	.89	1.19

Yellow Mixing Bowls

Deep, properly shaped, highly glazed, yellow earthenware mixing bowls, decorated with three embossed white lines encircling center. Sanitary and easy to clean. Set contains five bowls, one each, 5, 6, 7, 8 and 9 inches. You'll find many uses for them. Ship. wt., per set, about 14 pounds.
5C105A............ 95c

Yellow earthenware bowls decorated with daisy design in green. For mixing, baking or for use on the table. Have greater capacity than ordinary mixing bowl. Set consists of 5 bowls, one each, 4, 5, 6, 7 and 8 inches. Ship. wt., about 13 lbs.
5C127A............ 95c

Set of Five Glass Mixing Bowls
Easy to wash and sanitary. Deep and shaped well for mixing. Set consists of five bowls, one each of 5, 6, 7, 8 and 9-inch size, a right size for any size batch. Ship. wt., about 15 lbs.
5C109A Set of 5 bowls 67c

7-Piece Berry Set

Seven-piece Berry Set of clear, highly polished, heavy pressed glass with scalloped edges and beautiful machine cut floral pattern and band. Set consists of 8-inch deep bowl and six 4-inch deep fruit dishes. Ship. wt., about 6 lbs.
5C256A............ 98c

5C171A Set of 12 light weight pressed, 8 oz., tumblers. Ship. wt., 4 lbs............ 43c

5C172A Set of 12 light blown,pear optic 8 oz., tumblers. Ship. weight............ 53c

5C173A Set of 12 heavy pressed, 10 oz., tumblers. Ship. wt., 7 lbs............ 51c

Genuine Crackle Finish
Beautiful light blown glass, 7-piece water set, in the famous "Jack Frost" genuine crackle ware. A dainty set, suitable for use on any occasion, that is very economical in price. Set consists of novel squat pitcher and six 8-ounce tumblers. Can be shipped by parcel post. Ship. wt., about 8 lbs.
5C125A Per set $1.15

Nut or Sauce Bowl

9-inch pressed glass, Footed Nut or Sauce Bowl. Of fire polished handsomely figured clear glass. Ornamental and useful as a table decoration. A bargain. Ship. weight, about 3½ lbs.
5C112A Each............ 39c

Relish Dish

A dish, with cover, partitioned into three separate compartments, making it possible to serve several relishes in one dish. Made of highly polished clear crystal glass. Ship. wt., 3 lbs.
5C167A 39c

Grape Juice Set   8 Pieces $1.59

5C250A Some drinks are more appealing when taken from small attractive glasses. This set consisting of 11-inch bottle, six footed glasses and serving tray, makes a decorative buffet piece as well as to fulfill the need for the proper glass at the right time. Made of polished pressed glass with floral pattern. Ship. wt., 10 lbs. $1.59

Attractive Water Set

A most popular water set in clear pressed glass decorated with a design reproducing a famous cut glass pattern. Matches 5C256A Berry Set. Seven-piece set consists of attractive tankard pitcher, with scalloped edge, and six tumblers. Ship. wt., about 11 lbs.
5C255A............ $1.19

7

Decorated Glassware

The articles illustrated are from our D'Or Studios.

The glass is a rich cobalt blue, decorated in raised colored enamel. The decoration is a Spanish Caravel of the 15th Century. The border is finished in coin gold and decorated with seagulls in white enamel. The line is moderately priced and extremely effective.

Write for quotations.

GEO.
BORGFELDT
& CO.

16th Street and Irving Place
NEW YORK

a "loop," a "heart" and a myriad of other shapes. Within the "stirrup" style, there are subtle variations from plant to plant.

The point of this discussion is simple, yet complex: each glass factory had its own favorites in shape and style, but similar products from different factories will display distinct differences in detail. These detail differences allow one to identify the maker of a particular product. We have studied the shapes of sandwich tray handles and candy jar finials very carefully, and our study and comparisons have often been guided by sketches and correspondence from the files of the National Association of Manufacturers of Pressed and Blown Glassware (1893-1951).

The Roaring '20s and the Depression Era were punctuated by innovative colors in glass. At the same time, crystal (particularly elegant stemware) was also exceptionally popular and in great demand. This book is mostly about the colors made during these two decades, but some attention is given to crystal in the accounts of individual factories. However, color takes center stage! Those who think that "green and pink" constitute the whole of American glass from this period have much to see and learn in this book!

Who can resist the wonderful color names from this period? How many of these can you link these colors with their manufacturers? Bermuda Green, Cheriglo, Ebonite, Golden Green, Moongleam, Peachblo, Primrose, Russet, Sahara, or Venetian Red (just to mention a very few!). Even within this rainbow of color, some plants maintained their economic well-being by simply concentrating on opaque white glass (the Beaumont Company) or on black glass (the L. E. Smith Glass Company).

Beyond colors in glass, one encounters a splendid variety of decorations. These range from the simple elegance of applied gold or silver bands to elaborate handpainted floral motifs. In addition, by the late 1920s, several enterprises (particularly the Indiana Glass company, the Lancaster Glass Company and the Westmoreland Glass Company) had discovered that crystal glass, when completely covered by sprayed-on paint and augmented with additional trim or decorating, would sell! Many of these products, especially those of the Indiana and Lancaster concerns, have not been shown in full color until the publication of this book.

Sometimes, it's tempting to think of the October, 1929, stock market crash as a sharp dividing point between the Roaring '20s and the Depression Era of the 1930s. To do so would not do justice to history. Equally unjust is the thought that glassware produc-

tion technology suddenly changed from handmade to automatic machine. Those plants which converted some of their operations to semi-automatic or automatic machinery did so gradually, but new plants were sometimes built specifically for machine-made glass procedures. Some plants which flourished in the 1920s lacked the capital for great expansion in the 1930s.

The full story of glass tableware covering these two important decades cannot be told in a single volume, of course. There are several books to consult for more general information about glassware from the 1920s and the Depression Era. Among them are these: Hazel Marie Weatherman's' *Colored Glassware of the Depression Era* (first edition, 1969; second edition, 1970) and *Colored Glassware of the Depression Era 2* (1974); Tom and Neila Bredehoft's *Fifty Years of Collectible glass 1920-1970, Volume 1: Tableware, Kitchenware, Barware and Water Sets* (1997); *Warman's Depression Glass: A Value & Identification Guide* (1997), edited by Ellen T. Schroy; and, last but not least, Gene Florence's Collector's *Encyclopedia of Depression Glass*, which is now in its thirteenth edition (1998).

This book would not have been possible without the assistance of those who loaned glass for photography or provided important information through correspondence or their published writings. Our thanks to all of them: Doug and Margaret Archer; Cynthia and Roy Ash; Bud Ashmore; Michele Binetti; Bill Crowl; Frank M. Fenton; Dorothy Frayzee; Brad Geogeon; Marg Iwen; Jack and Dorothy Jordan; Lucile Kennedy; Willard Kolb; Lorraine Kovar; Addie Miller; Elizabeth Peters; Kay Riley; Elizabeth Northwood Robb; Christine Roberts; Dean Six; and Charles West Wilson. We owe a particularly large debt to Frank M. Fenton for his help in making the archives of the National Association of Manufacturers of Pressed and Blown Glassware (1893-1951) available to us.

As some of the foregoing pages have demonstrated, mere words cannot adequately capture the breadth, depth and variety of American glassware production during the 1920s and the Depression Era. For that reason, this book is mostly pictures. There are nearly a hundred color plates, and over 1100 individual items are pictured. For the most part, the products of various factories are grouped together, although some occasional direct comparisons of competitors' products are made on a particular page. Captions are at the bottom of each color page.

James Measell
Berry Wiggins
May 1998

BARTLETT-COLLINS GLASS COMPANY
SAPULPA, OKLAHOMA

H. U. BARTLETT, PRES.
D. C. HAMILTON, VICE PRES.
J. W. COLLINS, SECY.
E. E. BARTLETT, TREAS. & GEN. MGR.

DIRECTORS

H. E. WHITEHEAD
H. U. BARTLETT
H. A. McCAULEY
W. C. COLEMAN
J. W. COLLINS
D. C. HAMILTON
E. E. BARTLETT

HIGH CLASS
TABLE GLASSWARE
LAMPS, ETC.

THE BARTLETT-COLLINS GLASS CO.
MANUFACTURERS

SAPULPA, OKLA.

May 26th, 1925.

The Bartlett-Collins firm began about 1914, well after the petering out of the Ohio-Indiana-Illinois gas boom of the late nineteenth century had pushed some glass entrepreneurs to the west in search of fuel supplies. The Bartlett-Collins enterprise was one of the very few tableware firms west of the Mississippi River, although there were numerous bottle-making companies.

The company produced a good deal of hand-made tableware in the 1920s, ranging from pattern glass items to blown pitchers and tumblers (sold typically as ice tea sets) as well as stemware that could certainly qualify as "elegant" in the eyes of today's collectors. Some of these products are shown in Weatherman's *Colored Glassware of the Depression Era 2*.

By the early 1930s, Bartlett-Collins was moving more and more toward automated production. Ads for machine-made tumblers were frequent. These were typically decorated, but the motifs ranged from various bands to "characters" from popular radio programs like Major Bowes and movie cartoons. By the outset of WWII, the company had moved to machine production.

These thin-wall blown tumblers are decorated with characters from the Major Bowes Amateur Hour, a popular radio program of the 1930s (the colors used in this decoration are not known).

Timed to the Times—
Smart Glassware for Smart People

It is considered smart nowadays for the perfect host or hostess to serve cocktails and other beverages to guests in highly decorated glassware. We were pioneers in producing this type of ware. Illustrated are four of our good numbers in our No. 541 line. Reading from left to right they are: 1½-oz.—Decoration No. 4 in red, yellow and black; 7½-oz.—Decoration No. 7 in platinum; 10-oz.—Decoration No. 9, matt bands set off with red and yellow, and green and black; 12-oz.—Decoration No. 5 in red, yellow and black.

There was such a big demand for the 7½-oz. size upon its introduction that at the request of many customers we added the 1½-oz. and 10-oz. numbers and then, as an experiment, brought out the novel 12-oz. "Jumbo" size. It is surprising how well it has taken. It's a hit! All the items have heavy sham bottoms and are obtainable in other decorations besides those illustrated, including the No. 6 "Old Fashioned" group and the No. 8 "Cockerel." Made to sell on sight at popular prices. Write for quotations. All are packed three dozen to carton.

BARTLETT-COLLINS COMPANY
SAPULPA, OKLA.

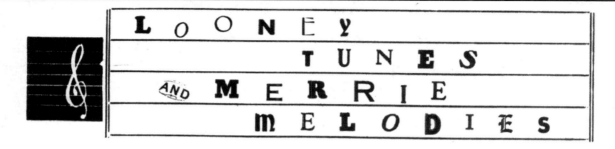

Another Bartlett-Collins Hit

■ It gives us great pleasure to announce that we have just completed arrangements with Leon Schlesinger for the exclusive right of decorating glassware on all subjects within the range of Looney Tunes and Merrie Melodies as created by him.

■ This new series of decorated tumblers shows the Looney Tunes done in a simple one color decoration and the Merrie Melodies in two colors and banded. All are popular priced sellers.

■ The line will be on display by all our sales representatives early in the year and a special showing will be made in **room 366, Hotel Pennsylvania** during the **New York China and Housewares Show,** January 24th to 30th.

BARTLETT-COLLINS COMPANY
SAPULPA, OKLAHOMA

THE BEAUMONT COMPANY
MORGANTOWN, WEST VIRGINIA

The Beaumont Company

MAIN OFFICE
MORGANTOWN, W. VA. 26505

JAMES B. KILSHEIMER III
PRESIDENT

The Beaumont Company's namesake, Percy J. Beaumont, emigrated to the United States from England in 1882. He was accompanied by his sister, Clara Elizabeth Beaumont, the fiance' of Harry Northwood. Beaumont worked for Hobbs-Brockunier in Wheeling, and he stayed with that firm when it became part of the United States Glass Company combine in the early 1890s.

About 1894-95, Beaumont started a glass decorating firm in the old Northwood factory in Martins Ferry, Ohio. Glass was also made there for a few years, but the enterprise relocated to Grafton, West Virginia, in 1902. When this plant changed hands in 1906, Beaumont went to Morgantown as manager of the Union Stopper Company. This organization was renamed the Beaumont Company in 1918, and Percy J. Beaumont served as vice-president and general manager for many years; he died in 1947. His eldest son, Arthur B. Beaumont, became involved in the organization about 1912 and ultimately served as president from 1953 to 1962.

Early on, the company focused much of its efforts on stationers' suppliers (inkwells, sponge cups, pen trays, etc.) but soon became involved in lighting goods. An opaque white glass called Fer-Lux was developed prior to World War I, and the Beaumont firm competed successfully with such lighting goods giants as Macbeth-Evans, which called its glass Alba.

Beaumont's opaque white glass was also used for tableware. The 1920s and the early 1930s witnessed a wide variety of tableware and other items, such as candleholders, vanity sets and boxes. Those from Beaumont's No. 148 line are hexagonal in shape, and they often feature inter-

esting decorative treatments, ranging from simple bands or colored dots to geometric designs or multi-colored effects. A graceful stork sometimes appears on vases (see Figs. 62 and 77), and one trade journal report (*Pottery, Glass and Brass Salesman*, November 29, 1928) mentions a butterfly decoration.

Crystal ware was sometimes satin finished or decorated with red edges and etching treatments similar to Fenton's. Beaumont's transparent green was often satin finished. An opaque jade green was also produced as were a vivid ruby and a noteworthy cobalt blue.

In the fall of 1936, the Beaumont firm notified the National Association of Manufacturers of Pressed and Blown Glassware that it was no longer making opaque white glass. Until this book, only a few of these products have been credited to Beaumont (see Cynthia Ash's article, "Ferlux: Beaumont's Mystery Glass," in the April/May, 1997, issue of *Glass Collector's Digest*)

The Beaumont firm closed relatively recently. The Fenton Art Glass Company bought a number of moulds, including those for lighting glassware, and some of the Beaumont's skilled workers found employment at Fenton.

CAMBRIDGE GLASS COMPANY
CAMBRIDGE, OHIO

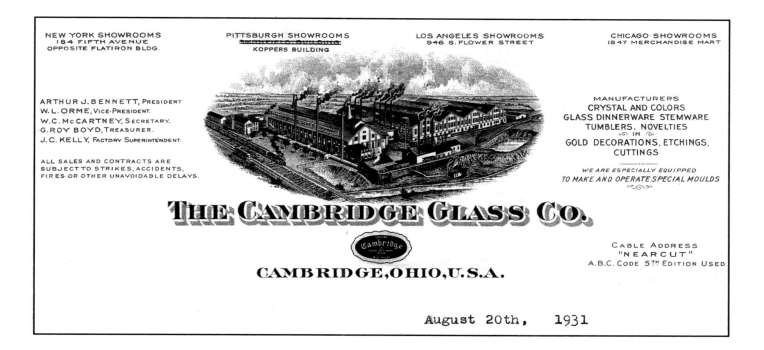

The large and important plant began when the National Glass Company combine (a Pittsburgh-based organization which controlled nineteen plants in Indiana, Maryland, Ohio, Pennsylvania and West Virginia) decided to build a new, modern plant in Cambridge, Ohio. Bonds were issued by a Pittsburgh bank to secure a $2 million mortgage, and construction began in 1901. Enthusiasm ran high, and one source predicted that 1000 to 1200 workers would be needed at the new plant.

In 1901, the Cambridge Glass Company was incorporated as a separate entity, but most of the National's kingpins were part of the enterprise. Moulds from other National plants were sent to Cambridge. The National began to suffer financial reverses in 1902, and a series of fires in various factories during 1903 led to receivership in 1904. A group of Cambridge-based investors, led by Arthur J. Bennett, purchased the plant from the nearly defunct National Glass Company in 1907. At this time, a line of imitation cut glass called "Near Cut" was selling well.

The 1920s and 1930s witnessed a kaleidoscope of colored glass from the Cambridge plant: Almond (1934), Amber (1924), Amber-glo (1926), Amethyst (1931), Avocado (c. 1927-28), Azurite (1922), Bluebell (1926), Carara (1923), Carmen (1931), cobalt blue (c. 1924-25), Coral (1935), Crown Tuscan (1932), Dianthus Pink (1934), Ebony (1922), Eleanor Blue (1933), Emerald (1923), Forest Green (1931), Gold Krystol (1929), Heatherbloom (1931), Helio (1923), Ivory (1924), Jade (1924), LaRosa (1938), Madeira (1929), Mocha (1938), Moonlight (1936), Mulberry (1923), Peach-blo (1925), Pistachio (1938), Primrose (1923), Ritz Blue (c. 1928-29), Royal Blue (1931), Rubina (1925), Topaz (1923), Willow Blue (1928), and Windsor Blue (1937).

Some of these colors were short lived, but others, such as Crown Tuscan, were made for many years. Readers should consult the National Cambridge Collectors' excellent book *Colors in Cambridge Glass* (Paducah: Collector Books, 1984) for a careful explanation and comparisons of Cambridge colors. Other good sources are the 1927-1929 Cambridge catalogs and the 1930-1934 Cambridge catalogs (both of which are available in reprint form).

The large Cambridge plant made a great variety of products and decorated much of its ware, especially with deep plate etchings. Among the key lines of tableware during the 1920s and 1930s were these: Aero Optic, Decagon, Everglade, Gadroon

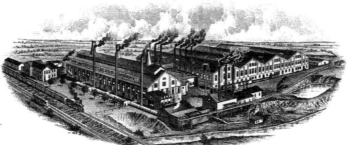

NEW YORK SHOWROOMS
184 FIFTH AVENUE
(OPPOSITE FLATIRON BLDG.)

ARTHUR J. BENNETT, PRESIDENT
W. L. ORME, VICE-PRESIDENT.
W. C. McCARTNEY, SECRETARY.
G. ROY BOYD, TREASURER.
J. C. KELLY, FACTORY SUPERINTENDENT.

ALL SALES AND CONTRACTS ARE
SUBJECT TO STRIKES, ACCIDENTS,
FIRES OR OTHER UNAVOIDABLE DELAYS.

CHICAGO SHOWROOMS

1547 MERCHANDISE MART

MANUFACTURERS
CRYSTAL AND COLORS
GLASS DINNERWARE STEMWARE
TUMBLERS, NOVELTIES
IN
GOLD DECORATIONS, ETCHINGS,
CUTTINGS.

WE ARE ESPECIALLY EQUIPPED
TO MAKE AND OPERATE SPECIAL MOULDS

THE CAMBRIDGE GLASS CO.

QUALITY
ORIGINALITY Ⓒ SALABILITY

CAMBRIDGE, OHIO, U.S.A.

ADDRESS ALL COMMUNICATIONS TO THE
COMPANY AT CAMBRIDGE, OHIO. THIS
SAVES DELAYS. PLEASE MARK REPLIES FOR

ATTENTION OF _____

CABLE ADDRESS
"NEARCUT"
A.B.C. CODE 5TH EDITION USED

October 7th, 1930

(3500), Martha Washington, Mount Vernon, Round Dinnerware (also called Cambridge Round), Tally-Ho (1402) and Wetherford.

The Cambridge Glass Company fell upon hard times in the 1950s, and, after a closure, it reopened as worker-owned stock company. It closed in 1958, and the moulds and other assets were sold to the Imperial Glass Corporation of Bellaire, Ohio, in 1960.

144.   Mustard and Cover.

**These pieces
(and those at the top of the next page)
are from Cambridge's No. 2800
"Community Crystal" line.**

103. High Foot Bowl and Cover.
Two Sizes.

104. High Foot Bowl and Cover on Plate.

98. 6½ inch Bowl.
99. 7½ inch Bowl.
100. 8½ inch Bowl.
A Round.

98. 7 inch Bowl.
99. 8 inch Bowl.
100. 9 inch Bowl.
D Shallow.

116. Footed Rose Bowl.
Three Sizes.

117. Lilly Bowl.
Three Sizes.

Top:
These pieces (and those on the previous page) are from Cambridge's No. 2800 "Community Crystal" line.

Below:
Note the shapes and colors in this ad from the mid-1920s.

105.   Low Foot Bowl and Cover on Plate.

101.   6 inch Low Foot Bowl, C Belled. also make
101.   6 inch, A Round.
101.   6½ inch, D Shallow.

HOLIDAY GIFTS

We offer for your trial a collection of EBONY and AZURITE glass with COIN GOLD DECORATED and EN-CRUSTED EDGES. These are all quick selling numbers and are articles that will bring you a good PROFIT.

Assortment

$65⁰⁰

or

$36⁰⁰

This package consists of 2 pieces each of the 14 items and 4 pieces of each Candlestick, making in all 36 pieces. The cost is $65.00 for the lot ready for shipment, f. o. b. Cambridge, Ohio. A smaller assortment or one-half the above quantity can be furnished at a price of $36.00.

Write us for full information on additional items in these lines

The Cambridge Glass Co.
Cambridge, Ohio, U. S. A.

19

CENTRAL GLASS COMPANY
WHEELING, WEST VIRGINIA

This enterprise was founded in the early 1860s, and, by 1867, it was known as the Central Glass Company. John Oesterling and Nathan B. Scott were the key figures in the firm's early history. In 1891, the Central plant became "Factory O" of the United States Glass Company combine. Within several years, the plant was idled due to financial and labor problems in the combine, but a group led by Nathan B. Scott bought the plant from the U. S. Glass Company and reopened it as the Central Glass Company.

In 1919, the Central firm purchased the moulds for the entire line of Chippendale pattern ware which had been made and marketed successfully by the Jefferson Glass Company of Follansbee, West Virginia, for about a decade (incidentally, the Jefferson had earlier acquired these moulds from the Ohio Flint Glass Company of Lancaster, Ohio). The Central also bought the right to use the Jefferson's registered "Krys-tol" trade-mark in conjunction with Chippendale. Large quantities of the pressed line were exported to England, but the Chippendale line also remained popular in the United States.

The Central made Chippendale throughout the 1920s, but other products were also developed. Several console sets were marketed; these were

THE HOUSE OF QUALITY
Central Glass Works
WHEELING, W. VA.

DOOR PORTER,
Seven inches tall. Weight 2½ lbs.

New lines now on display for 1916 at our

BRANCH OFFICES:
NEW YORK .... 66 W. Broadway
PHILADELPHIA .... 610 Denckla Bldg.
BALTIMORE .... 33 S. Charles St.
BOSTON .... 157 Summer St.
CINCINNATI .... 14 Blymer Bldg.
BUFFALO .... 700 Main St.
SAN FRANCISCO .... 718 Mission St.

Palmer House, Chicago, Ill., Jan. 9th to Feb. 9th, 1916, T. H. Butcher in charge.

H. HAZLETT, PRES.   A. S. HARE, VICE-PRES.   EDW. J. SCHAUB, SEC'Y & TREAS.   J. CECIL FEE, GEN. MGR.

A. B. C. CODE-CHIPPENDALE
(5TH EDITION)

CENTRAL GLASS WORKS
WHEELING WEST VIRGINIA

MANUFACTURERS OF

CHIPPENDALE
"KRYS-TOL"
THE GLASS OF QUALITY

PRESSED

August
9
1927

The Old
Central
Quality

BLOWN

often decorated crystal featuring orange or blue, and the look reminds one of similar ware made by Indiana, Lancaster or Westmoreland. Central also made these console sets in opalescent glass.

A few pattern lines, such as No. 2010, were made in colors (amber, green and pink), but the Central concentrated strongly on blown stemware. These were top-notch products, and the firm often advertised them in conjunction with the slogan "The Old Central Quality." Pressed ware for beverage service also assumed an increasingly stronger role in the Central's fortunes.

Prohibition took its toll on this plant's production of bar ware, and the Depression exacerbated its financial problems. The factory shut down for a time in 1932-33, and it never fully regained its strength when it started up once more. In 1939, a number of moulds and some other fixtures were sold to the Imperial Glass Corporation across the Ohio River in Bellaire, Ohio.

No. 2000 Console Set— 10-in. Comport, 9-in. Candlesticks

Chippendale KrysTol

Console Set made in Celeste Blue, Mirror Black, Amethyst, Green, Canary and Chinese Jade, also in flat and paste gold encrustations.

CENTRAL GLASS WORKS
Wheeling, W. Va.

The Old Central Quality In New Modernistic Designs

We have reproduced a few items of our 2010 Line—made in pleasing shades of Rose, Green and Amber. Other items in this and our various lines of Blown and Pressed Ware in exclusive shapes and designs will be on display in Pittsburgh, Pa., at Wm. Penn Hotel, Room 811, January 7th to 19th, inclusive.

CENTRAL GLASS WORKS, Wheeling, W. Va. ROBERT L. HUTCHISON

Fruit-Bowl given for **Four** Subscriptions

Console-Set
Given Complete for Six Subscriptions

Candlesticks given for **Four** Subscriptions

THIS attractive console-set when used on the buffet will add an artistic touch of dignity to the dining-room. These sets have become very popular, and in the choice of colors which we offer, one can surely find a most suitable and proper buffet-decoration. We offer you your choice of **Sapphire, Amethyst** and **Canary**—beautiful deep shades of these colors which have been perfected only after years of costly experiment. This set consists of a fruit-bowl nine inches in diameter and about 4½-inches high upon its separate black base, and a pair of 7-inch candlesticks in the artistic shape shown in the illustration. Be sure to state choice of color, and when ordering set complete, please mention **Gift No. 2554.**

Many of our readers will want to order the bowl or candlesticks separately, and we shall be glad to furnish either the bowl or the pair of candlesticks for four subscriptions. The extra subscription is to cover cost of separate packing. In ordering the bowl, mention **Gift No. 2555.** In ordering the pair of candlesticks, mention **Gift No. 2556.**

*This Beautiful Console Set is
One of the Amber and White Opalescent Items*

Our New Opalescent Line
Is One of the Season's Hits

The first of the year we uncovered at the Pittsburgh Show among our novelties a new Amber and White Opalescent line of fancy glassware. Its charm both by reason of the appearance of the metal and the beautiful shapes typically Central products made it a big hit and we feel confident in recommending it to the trade.

Co-Operative Flint Glass Company, Ltd.
Beaver Falls, Pennsylvania

CABLE ADDRESS
"FLINTGLASS" BEAVER FALLS, PA.

Co-Operative Flint Glass Co.

Beaver Falls, Pa. December 31 1926

C.W. KLEIN
SECRETARY AND TREASURER

This history of this interesting firm goes back to late 1860s when a glass plant operated in Beaver Falls. In the late 1870s, a group of glassworkers (who were on strike at the McKee plant in Pittsburgh) founded the Co-Operative Flint Glass Company, Ltd. The firm prospered during the 1880s and 1890s, making pattern glass and lamps. The company remained independent of the United States Glass Company and the National Glass Company, the two combines organized in the 1890s.

The October, 1904, issue of *Glass and Pottery World* described the Co-Op's products as "a line of fish globes, aquariums, cake covers, seed cups, sample bottles, etc. in such infinite variety as to astonish one not familiar with the vast quantities of such goods produced." A fire in January, 1906, caused considerable damage, but the plant was rebuilt and the enterprise continued to prosper.

In the 1920s, the Co-Operative firm produced a wide variety of products. The January 15, 1923, issue of *China, Glass and Lamps* mentioned "console sets, comports, flower bowls, vases, baskets, bulb bowls, candlesticks, salad plates and other staple and novelty shapes," but there were also candy jars, luncheon sets and ashtrays. The No. 481 7" candlestick, made in a three-part mould, is quite similar to those made by the Central and Northwood firms, but the latter were made in two-part moulds. The Adoria pattern was available in numerous articles. The interesting Lace Edge ware was also in vogue, and a plain line called Martha Washington, which was introduced about 1912, continued in production.

Colors included these: amber, amethyst, aquamarine blue, Midnight Black, cobalt blue, canary,

No. 462
Candy Jar and Cover

This plain candy jar was made in a wide variety of colors during the 1920s.

Black glass was especially popular in the late 1920s.

No. 537 Sweetmeat, 10½ inch

This unusually-shaped sweetmeat dish was shown as an "unknown" in Weatherman's
Colored Glassware of the Depression Era 2.

green, rose, ruby and the unusual yellow-orange-red Sunset hue (this was introduced in 1924-25; see Roy Ash's "Co-Operative Flint's Sunset Glass" in the August/September, 1994, issue of *Glass Collector's Digest*). Decorating treatments ranged from cutting to a most attractive amber stain, which was prominently featured on the Adoria pattern line as well as some console sets .

After the Co-Operative Flint closed about 1937, many of its moulds (ranging from 1880s patterns to c. 1930 wares) were purchased and utilized by the Phoenix Glass Company.

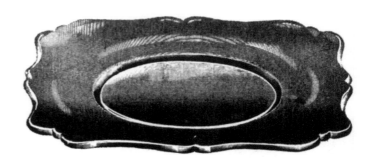

Square plate in black glass, c. 1929.

Aug. 23, 1927.

R. C. COBLE

FLOWER BLOCK

Filed May 3, 1927

Des. 73,280

Fig 1

Design patent for an unusual flower block.

CO-OPERATIVE FLINT
GLASS CO.
Beaver Falls, Pa.
Manufacturers of
Blown and Pressed Glassware
IN CRYSTAL AND COLORS
for
Jobbers Assortments — Soda Fountains
Hotel and Restaurant Trade
and all
Departments looking for specialties for gifts as well
as useful and staple items.

Our Latest Creation.
ALL GLASS 31 PIECE LUNCHEON SET
in
Amber — Green — Amethyst and Canary

Complete Line Will Be Shown
During January Exhibit, Ft.
Pitt Hotel, Pittsburgh.
Rooms 135-136-137
W. A. Reaper
In Charge.

DAVIES GLASS AND MANUFACTURING COMPANY
MARTINS FERRY, OHIO

Not much is known about this short-lived firm, but the enterprise made at least one significant item, an unusual footed sandwich tray with a center handle (a traditional sandwich tray was also produced, and both of these are illustrated in this book).

During the summer of 1920, *Crockery and Glass Journal* reported that "contracts have been awarded by the Davies Glass Co. of Martins Ferry, O., for the erection of a new plant." The site near the Ohio River was the ruins of the former Haskins Glass Company, which had burned in 1909. The Davies organization was prepared to invest about $100,000 in buildings and equipment, and the *Journal* predicted that "manufacturing will start before the end of the year."

Another trade journal report in early 1921 noted the election of corporate officers but also said "it is expected that this new factory will be ready for operations during the coming spring." The company officers were listed as follows: Thomas W. Pursglove, president; E. K. Hoge, vice-president; A. J. Fallen, secretary; and W. E. Thomas, treasurer. W. W. Davies completed the board of directors.

When in operation, the firm's plant had a 16 pot furnace, so the potential for quantity production

seems to have existed. Unfortunately, correspondence between the Davies organization and the National Association of Manufacturers of Pressed and Blown Glassware mentions only a few products, such as pressed stoppers, a night bottle and a pressed lens.

The center handle sandwich tray was in production during 1923-24 (this sandwich tray is also known with a distinctive leaf pattern on its underside). The No. 2 Footed Sandwich Tray made its debut in January, 1924, and a full-page advertisement appeared in *Pottery, Glass and Brass Salesman* (see next page). The firm's general manager, Ira M. Clarke, was also associated with the New Martinsville Glass Manufacturing Company at this time.

The Davies concern made crystal glass, and this is sometimes found decorated or with attractive light cutting work, but it is not known whether Davies did this or sold its wares as blanks. The ad in *Pottery, Glass and Brass Salesman* mentions that Davies' glass is "particularly desirable for cutters or decorators," so it might have been sold as blanks.

The only Davies' colors documented so far are amber and an interesting opaque red that is similar to both Fenton's Venetian Red and Northwood's Chinese Coral, each of which was in production about 1924-25.

On June 3, 1926, a glass trade publication reported that the Davies' plant "has been idle for over a year." It did not reopen.

Postcard of Davies Glass House in Martins Ferry, Ohio , ca. 1921.

No. 2 Footed Sandwich Tray

In Honor of 1924's Birthday!

Here is one of the items that will help the Davies factory make history in 1924. Note the graceful lines of tray itself and the simple but sturdy character of the foot. The handle, as Polonius would say, is "neat but not gaudy." Like our other products it is made of an excellent quality of pot glass. It is particularly desirable for cutters or decorators.

Entire new line on show in Room 621

Fort Pitt Hotel, Pittsburgh

JANUARY 7th to 26th

Ira M. Clarke, General Manager, in Charge

DAVIES GLASS & MFG. COMPANY

Martin's Ferry, Ohio

Frederick Skelton, New York Representative, 200 Fifth Avenue

Diamond Glass-Ware Company
Indiana, Pennsylvania

The roots of the Diamond Glass-Ware Company's plant go deep in Indiana, Pennsylvania. In 1892, the Indiana Glass Company constructed a factory, but this enterprise failed, and town boosters sought an experienced glassmaker to revive it. They found Harry Northwood, an English emigrant who, although only 36 years old, had wide experience in the glass tableware industry. He headed The Northwood Company at Indiana from 1896 until late 1899 when the plant became part of the National Glass company combine.

Under the National's aegis, the Indiana-based plant was directed by Harry Bastow and Thomas E. A. Dugan. In early 1904, Dugan and his brother Alfred were able to purchase the operation from the National, and it flourished for nearly a decade as the Dugan Glass Co. Their iridescent glassware competed successfully with similar products being made by Fenton, Imperial, Millersburg and Northwood. About 1913, the Dugan men left after a dispute with the other investors, and the organization was soon reconstituted as the Diamond Glass Company. By early 1916, Alfred Dugan had returned to Indiana as glassmaker and plant manager, posts he held until his death in 1928.

The firm was known as the Diamond Glass-Ware Company from 1916 on, and it ceased operations after a disastrous fire on June 27, 1931. The factory itself was not badly damaged and the moulds were intact, but the offices, decorating area, packing room and warehouses had been destroyed. There were efforts to rebuild, but the company went into receivership and some fixtures and moulds were sold to the Fenton Art Glass Company. In 1939, L. G. "Si" Wright purchased glassmaking tools and moulds, some of which dated back to the 1890s.

Between 1920 and 1931, the Diamond Glass-Ware Co. made a wide variety of products. Iridescent ware dominated the first half of the 1920s with such lines as Rainbow Lustre, Golden Lustre, Egyptian Lustre and Royal Lustre. Egyptian Lustre was made with black glass, and Royal Lustre featured an extraordinarily vivid, mirror-like iridescence on blue glass. Diamond also made an opaque jade green and an opaque red which is similar to Fenton's Venetian Red and Northwood's Chinese Coral, both of which were in production about 1924-25.

In 1925, the Diamond introduced its No. 900 line, which is known as Adam's Rib by collectors today. No. 900 was made in amber, blue, green and pink as well as iridescent blue (see Figs. 192-206). Articles are frequently decorated with gold bands or "hammered gold" in addition to black paint which may be augmented with handpainted floral motifs.

The Diamond plant was involved in creating one Spanish-style line, Barcelona, which debuted in 1928. It proved to be less popular than its competitors' wares, however, and was soon discontinued.

The Diamond's last major line was called Victory, and it was produced from the summer of 1928 until the plant's demise about three years later. Victory was made in several transparent colors--amber, royal blue, green and pink--as well as opaque black. The line began with the typical luncheon sets, but its popularity spurred the introduction of these items: goblet, sherbet, mayonnaise bowl, grapefruit bowl, soup plate, gravy boat, cream soup, pickle dish, oval vegetable dish and comports of various sizes.

For more information on Diamond glass, readers should consult *Dugan/Diamond: The Story of Indiana, Pennsylvania Glass* (Antique Publications, 1993).

DUNCAN-MILLER GLASS COMPANY
WASHINGTON, PENNSYLVANIA

This long-lived, successful firm began as George Duncan & Sons in Pittsburgh in the mid-1870s. The factory became part of the United States Glass Company combine and was known as "Factory D." It was badly damaged by fire in 1892, and the principals (Harry B. Duncan; James E. Duncan, Sr.; and John E. Miller) left the combine and built a new plant at Washington, Pennsylvania. About the turn of the century, it was known as the Duncan & Miller Glass Company. Later it became known simply as Duncan-Miller, often without the hyphen.

From the mid-1920s through most of the 1930s, Duncan Miller introduced major pattern lines regularly. These can be briefly summarized as follows: 1924, No. 40 ("Spiral Flutes"); 1925-26, Early American Sandwich No. 41; 1928, Georgian No. 103; 1929, Puritan; 1929-30, Hobnail No. 110; 1931, No. 21 ("Punties"); 1932, No. 126 Venetian; 1933, No. 75 Whitney; 1934, No. 128 (Sculptured Glass satin finished) and No. 301 Tear Drop; and 1935, Terrace.

The two most significant Duncan Miller pattern are probably No. 110 Hobnail and Early American Sandwich No. 41. Variations on the hobnail motif were later to dominate the American glass tableware scene, but Duncan Miller was among the first to be in the marketplace with a hobnail line. Early American Sandwich caught the fancy of the buying public, and it remained in the Duncan Miller line for many, many years.

Duncan Miller colors are almost as noteworthy as the pattern lines. The firm made the standard green and pink (Rose), of course, but both dark blue (Royal blue) and light blue (Sapphire Blue) were produced along with black, an excellent ruby, and a shade called Carmen.

In the mid-1950s, the plant was acquired by the U. S. Glass Co., and moulds were moved to the Glassport, Pa., branch of the U. S. firm. In the

1960s, some of these moulds were purchased by the Fenton Art Glass Company of Williamstown, West Virginia. This purchase included moulds for many different articles, and some of them are currently in the Fenton line.

Oct. 1, 1935. R. A. MAY Des. 97,082

ARTICLE OF GLASSWARE OR SIMILAR ARTICLE

Filed Jan. 25, 1935

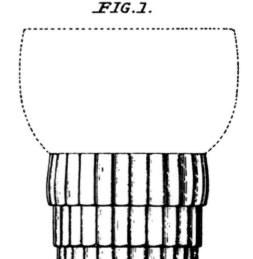

FIG.1.

Duncan Glass Co., Washington, Pa.

March 5, 1940. R. A. MAY **Des. 119,280**

TUMBLER OR SIMILAR ARTICLE

Filed Dec. 21, 1939

March 5, 1940. R. A. MAY **Des. 119,278**

TUMBLER OR SIMILAR ARTICLE

Filed Dec. 21, 1939

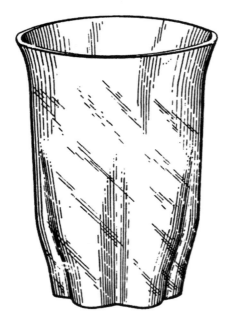

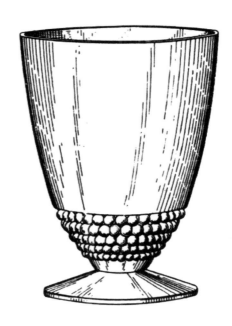

LACE GLASS

—a breath of early New England

Rich in the traditions of Sandwich, the famous old Cape Cod glassmaking center, this stately design—our No. 41 Line—presents its appeal to every lover of fine glassware.

Here is reproduced the same sparkling brilliancy with its illusion of delicate frost work, spread like a shimmering lace veil over its gleaming surface. Designs that follow the best traditions. Pieces of utility, remarkable for their outstanding beauty, such as salad plates, dessert saucers, compotes, grapefruits, sundaes, goblets, sherbets and sherbet plates, etc.

Crystal and two delicate colors — amber and green.

The
Duncan & Miller Glass Co.
Washington, Pa.

REPRESENTATIVES:

Paul Joseph, 200 Fifth Avenue, New York.
Murt Wallace, 157 Summer St., Boston, Mass.
F. L. Renshaw, 30 E. Randolph St., Chicago, Ill.
Joseph Tomkinson, 1104 Arch St., Philadelphia.
Harry T. Thomas & Co., 29 S. Hanover St., Baltimore, Md.
Marsh & Kidd, 617 Mission St., San Francisco, Cal.
E. B. Hill, Factory Representative, Washington, Pa.

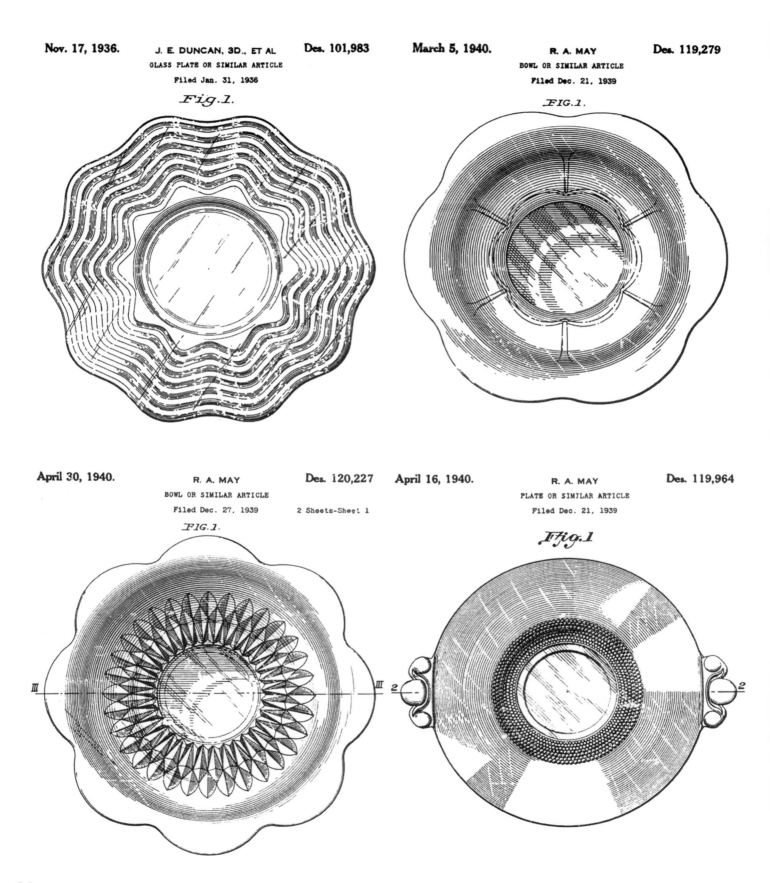

Nov. 17, 1936.   J. E. DUNCAN, 3D., ET AL   Des. 101,983

GLASS PLATE OR SIMILAR ARTICLE

Filed Jan. 31, 1936

Fig.1.

March 5, 1940.   R. A. MAY   Des. 119,279

BOWL OR SIMILAR ARTICLE

Filed Dec. 21, 1939

FIG.1.

April 30, 1940.   R. A. MAY   Des. 120,227

BOWL OR SIMILAR ARTICLE

Filed Dec. 27, 1939   2 Sheets-Sheet 1

FIG.1.

April 16, 1940.   R. A. MAY   Des. 119,964

PLATE OR SIMILAR ARTICLE

Filed Dec. 21, 1939

Fig.1

34

DUNBAR GLASS CORPORATION
DUNBAR, WEST VIRGINIA

Although it operated for about four decades (1913-1953), this is one of those elusive companies about which not much is known. Originally called the "Dunbar Flint Glass Corporation," the firm shortened its name about 1930. Company catalogs reveal a complex product numbering system in which numerical designations are not standard and often change solely because of the color or decoration. The Dunbar products shown in this book appear in either factory catalogs or Butler Brothers assortments.

Iridescent ware (always called "lustre" or "luster") was a Dunbar staple for many years. Unlike the earlier Carnival glass (popular from 1908-1920), which was made by spraying hot glass, Dunbar's lustre ware was produced by applying a liquid solution to finished glassware at room temperature and then placing the articles in a decorating lehr or kiln. This procedure allows the decorator to coat areas of the piece with the lustre treatment while other portions remain untreated. These Dunbar lustre colors were mentioned in trade journal ads or notes over the years: "red, yellow, blue, rose, pearl, and lavender" (1924); amber, wine, blue iridescent and peach (1926); Light Amber, Gunmetal blue, Garden Green, and Amethyst (1935).

Decorated ware was featured in the Dunbar line, and these products were mentioned at various times: "a perfect ... copy of the expensive Silver Deposit vases" (*Pottery, Glass and Brass Salesman*, December 3, 1925); "fancy glassware adorned with decalomania decorations" (1928); gold encrusted items with "Rambler Rose" decoration (1928); Antique Silvered glass (July, 1929); Brocatelle with a "beautiful engraved finish" (1930); and sandblast squares with cut lines (1936)

A New York sales office was opened in the Onyx Building (24th and Broadway) during June, 1928. At this time, J. M. Payne, Jr., was Dunbar's president, and H. F. Phillips was sales manager. *Pottery, Glass and Brass Salesman* (November 22, 1928) reported that Dunbar was represented by the D. Saunders Company in Chicago, and these products were then on display: "Candy jars, console sets, nut bowl, hexagon cake salver on stand, and a heart-shaped candy dish are offered in a satin fin-

ish with floral designs in a hand-painted effect showing through. The brightly colored cherry pattern on rosine or green is proving a popular number for quick sales. The handpainting effect beneath the satin finish gives this line a smart touch that sets it off from the average glassware."

Crystal was prominent in the Dunbar offerings, but pink (sometimes called rose-pink) and green (sometimes called Bermuda green) were also mentioned with some frequency. Amber and ruby seem somewhat harder to find today.

Some of the products of the Dunbar enterprise are quite similar in style, color and decoration to many items made by companies in the Weston, West Virginia, area (see Dean Six's article, "Weston Glass," in the December/January, 1994, issue of *Glass Collector's Digest*). Furthermore, trade journal advertisements from the 1920s and 1930s show glassware which continued to be made throughout much of the 1940s and, quite probably, until the company's demise about 1953. No Dunbar products are shown in the 1998 fourth edition of Florence's *Collectible Glassware* from the 40s-50s-60s.

SET #137/D900
Assorted colored stripes
To retail for $1

SET #134
Cut Silver Rose
To retail for $1.95

SET #110
Six assorted lusters
To retail for $1.95

SET #147
Six assorted lusters
To retail for $1.79

Each set consists of one jug and six glasses—packed one set to a carton and six sets to a shipping carton.

These are just a few of the popular Dunbar Beverage Sets—there are many more in crystal, luster, stripes and hand treatments. Dunbar offers you the latest in style, utility and appeal—and at prices to allow an excellent mark-up.

Beverage Sets to retail at $1.⁰⁰ and up

3316

3319

3313

3317

3303

3315

3118-132

3314

3311

3310

3312

3318

No. 2555/12 in.   No. 2563 8 in.   No. 2556/6 in.   No. 2557 10 in.
$5.75 doz. $2.75 doz. $1.75 doz. $3.75 doz.

NO PACKING CHARGES

Not Silver Deposit—But Mighty Like!

Dunbar's Ice Tea Set Specials

in
CRYSTAL
LUSTRES
Amber, Wine, Blue
Iridescent

CRYSTAL
OR
LUSTRE
CUT

No. 8701 Tumbler and Coaster

No. 412 Tumbler and Coaster

PRICES AND SAMPLES SENT ON REQUEST

FULL LINE OF SAMPLES ON DISPLAY AT THE FOLLOWING SHOWROOMS

NEW YORK CITY E. W. Hammond 10 West 23rd Street	**BOSTON, MASS** Wm. R. Amidon 99 Bedford Street	**NEW ORLEANS, LA.** H. L. Thompson 703 Canal Street	**PORTLAND, OREG.** Eastern Manf. Co. 29 North Fifth Street
PHILADELPHIA, PA. John A. Nixon 906 Filbert Street	**CHICAGO, ILL.** D. Saunders & Co. 17 North Wabash Avenue	**CINCINNATI, OHIO** Carl A. Larson 519 Main Street	**DETROIT, MICH.** G. T. McCracken & Co. 315 Donovan Bldg.

DUNBAR FLINT GLASS CORP., DUNBAR, W. VA.

ECONOMY GLASS COMPANY
MORGANTOWN GLASS WORKS
MORGANTOWN, WEST VIRGINIA

This plant began as the Morgantown Glass Works in the late 1890s, but it changed its name to the Economy Tumbler Company in 1903. Two decades later, it became the Economy Glass Company, but it readopted the title Morgantown Glass Works on July 1, 1929. During the 1920s and part of the 1930s, the key executive was George Dougherty, a glassman of long experience who later became an officer of the National Association of Manufacturers of Pressed and Blown Glassware. The factory manager, Joseph Haden, was also a fixture at this firm.

As the name implied, the Economy Tumbler Co. focused its efforts on utilitarian glassware. Advertisements in *Pottery, Glass and Brass Salesman* during 1912 touted "high grade lead" glassware," and these products were listed: blown and pressed tumblers, stem ware, jugs, vases, decanters, beer mugs, oil bottles, water bottles, sugars and creams." These decorative treatments were mentioned: "light cuttings, enamel decorations, crests and monograms, needle etchings and deep plate etchings."

Earl W. Newton, the Economy's longstanding sales representative in Chicago, was instrumental in changing the firm's direction away from staples to higher quality stemware and specialties in transparent colors and crystal. An ambitious factory expansion in 1919 led to a plethora of colors during the 1920s and early 1930s--Aqua Marine, azure, black, green, Green Peacock Optic, jade, pastel green, Ritz Blue, Rose Marie, ruby, Spanish Red, Stiegel green, and topaz.

Among the Economy Glass Company's products in the 1920s was its No. 1500 line. Records from the files of the National Association of Manufacturers of Pressed and Blown Glassware list numerous pieces, but the first group was as follows: berry bowl, footed cup and saucer, footed creamer and sugar, tray, plates (6-inch, 8-inch and 12-inch) and sherbet. This was produced in crystal, green and iridescent ware, and sketches make clear that Economy's No. 1500 is the line called "Round Robin" by collectors today.

For more information about this company, readers should consult Jerry Gallagher's *Handbook of Old Morgantown Glass* (privately printed, 1995).

MORGANTOWN GLASS WORKS

MANUFACTURERS OF

HIGH GRADE  GLASSWARE

MORGANTOWN, W. VA.   July 8th,

Letterhead, c. 1930.

THE JEWELERS' CIRCULAR   March, 1931

SPARKLING GIFTS FOR SPRIGHTLY SALES!

THESE glass jars with their quaint knobbed covers will intrigue many feminine shoppers by their rich tones of Ruby, Ritz Blue or Black, enhanced by dancing lights from the cut crystal knobs. Though they are particularly attractive as candy jars, they may be used also to hold powder and a puff, or what you will.

MORGANTOWN GLASS WORKS
MORGANTOWN, W. VA.

—Sales Offices—

80 SUMMER ST., BOSTON
1007 FILBERT ST., PHILA.
308 W. RANDOLPH ST., CHICAGO
1604 ARAPAHOE ST., DENVER
731 FOLSOM ST., SAN FRANCISCO

200 FIFTH AVENUE, NEW YORK
110 HOPKINS PLACE, BALTIMORE
838 RAYMOND AVE., ST. PAUL
410 HOLLAND BLDG., SEATTLE
TRANSPORTATION BLDG., LOS ANGELES

Ultra-Modern LIQUOR SETS . . .
featuring Platinum Decoration at its best

No. 24-24 Decanter; No. 9719-3 Tumbler; platinum decorated rings.

No. 9719-12 Hi Ball; platinum decorated rings.

Here are six brilliant conceptions from the hands of expert designers—flawlessly blown in the famous Old Morgantown manner—decorated with bands of gleaming platinum that never lose their lustre (an exclusive Old Morgantown quality that will please your patrons).

Each "set" you sell will consist of a Bottle and Stopper, six Hi Ball Glasses and six Liquor Glasses (or a bottle with six glasses). Your choice of Black, Ritz Blue, Stiegel Green, Ruby or Crystal—with Crystal Stoppers. Attractive prices. Write us!

Old Morgantown
GLASSWARE

MORGANTOWN GLASS WORKS
Morgantown, W. Va.

No. 2 Decanter, P/D791
9051-1½ Tumbler, P/D791
8701-14 Hi Ball, P/D791

No. 10½ Bar Bottle, P/D Sparta
9051-1½ Tumbler, P/D Sparta
8071-14 Hi Ball, P/D Sparta

No. 10½ Bar Bottle, P/D Flora
9051-1½ Tumbler, P/D Flora
8071-14 Hi Ball, P/D Flora

No. 21-24 Decanter, P/D Roses
9051-1½ Tumbler, P/D Roses
8701-14 Hi Ball, P/D Roses

No. 10½ Bar Bottle, P/D Roses
9051-1½ Tumbler, P/D Roses
8701-14 Hi Ball, P/D Roses

41

Fenton Art Glass Company
Williamstown, West Virginia

From a modest beginning as a decorating firm in Martins Ferry, Ohio, in 1905, the Fenton Art Glass Company grew steadily and remained strong during the 1920s and 1930s when other glass plants failed or experienced great difficulties. Founded by brothers Frank L. Fenton and John W. Fenton, the company erected its plant in Williamstown in the fall of 1906 and made its first glass on January 2, 1907. John left the concern in 1909 to found the Millersburg Glass Company in Millersburg, Ohio.

The company was the originator of the iridescent glass now widely known as "Carnival glass," and production of this pressed ware in elaborate patterns dominated the 1908-1915 period of its history. After WWI, however, the enterprise broadened its scope dramatically. In 1928, a Fenton ad boasted that the firm had been in business 23 years and was then offering ware in 23 different colors!

During the 1920s, Fenton made iridescent ware in plain shapes and interesting colors, such as Wisteria (see Figs. 327-33), which was often spelled "Wistaria" in Fenton ads, and Tangerine. Other colors—such as Celeste Blue, Florentine Green, Grecian Gold, Persian Pearl, Topaz and Velva Rose—were in competition with similar shades made by Diamond and Northwood, among others.

Many of Fenton's opaque colors of the 1920s and 1930s were remarkably innovative. Their very names are evocative—Black, Cameo Opalescent, Chinese Yellow, Flame, Jade Green, Lilac, Mandarin Red, Mongolian Green, Moonstone, Pekin Blue, Periwinkle Blue and Venetian Red. Jacob Rosenthal

was both factory manager and glass chemist, and, when he became ill in 1927, he was succeeded by his son, Paul. Frank L. Fenton handled matters of design, and he was assisted by another Rosenthal son, Clarence, who headed the mould room.

(Text continued on page 47)

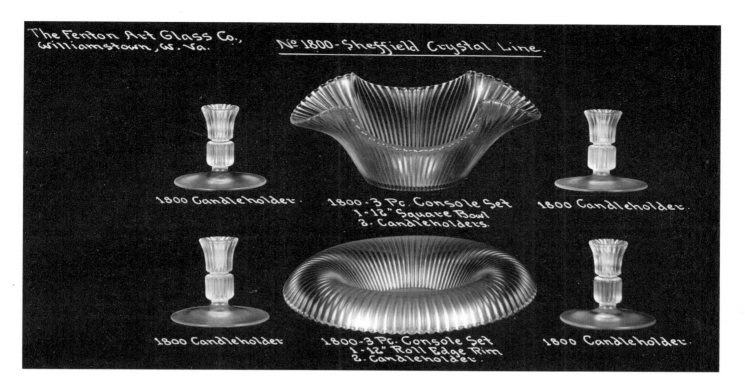

The Fenton Art Glass Co., Williamstown, W. Va.

No. 1800-Sheffield Crystal Line.

1800 Candleholder.

1800-3 Pc. Console Set
1-12" Square Bowl
2. Candleholders.

1800 Candleholder.

1800 Candleholder

1800-3 Pc. Console Set
1-12" Roll Edge Trim
2. Candleholder.

1800 Candleholder.

THE FENTON ART GLASS CO.
WILLIAMSTOWN, W. VA.
No. 1611 Georgian Tableware Line
Colors - Crystal - Green - Pink - Amber - Ruby - Royal Blue - Topaz - Black

No. 1611—2½ oz. Tumbler

No. 1611 Decanter

No. 1611—5 oz. Tumbler

No. 1611—10 oz. Tumbler

No. 1611 —½ Gal. Jug

No. 1611 — 8" Salad Plate
No. 1611 — 6" Salad Plate

No. 1611 Sherbet

No. 1611 Goblet

No. 1611—12 oz. Ice Tea

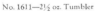

Fenton
FOR EVERY OCCASION

AT THE PITTSBURGH SHOW—ROOM 643—FORT PITT HOTEL

THE FENTON ART GLASS COMPANY
Williamstown, West Virginia

The 1930s were trying years for Fenton management, but the ability to make interesting colors and new patterns kept the firm in the black, albeit barely, when other companies were in receivership or faced bankruptcy. A Georgian pattern line was introduced in 1931 with the exotic name Agua Caliente, and it sold reasonably well, as did patterns such as Lincoln Inn, Plymouth and Sheffield. Decorative effects such as Halo, Ming, San Toy and Silvertone added to the firm's lines, too.

In 1938-39, skilled glassworker Pete Raymond was instrumental in developing techniques to "ring" the topmost edge of glass items with a contrasting color. The first such Fenton products, called Blue Ridge, featured French Opalescent glass with a cobalt blue edge. This innovation led to Fenton's production of many lines (Aqua Crest, Emerald Crest, Gold Crest, etc.) in the 1940s.

As the 1930s came to a close, Fenton was launching its Hobnail line. Hobnail was inspired by private mould mould work for the Allen B. Wrisley Company, a perfume manufacturer from Chicago.

For more information, readers should consult *Fenton Glass: The First Twenty-five Years* (1978) and *Fenton Glass: The Second Twenty-five Years* (1980), both of which are available from Antique Publications. Also helpful is Margaret and Kenn Whitmyer's *Fenton Art Glass, 1907-1939.*

FENTON'S NEW SHAPES AND COLORS *for 1939*

Peach Blow
Cranberry Red
Blue Ridge
Stiegel Blue
French and Green Opalescent

HAND/MADE IN AMERICA by Fenton

THE FENTON ART GLASS COMPANY
WILLIAMSTOWN, W. VA., U.S.A.

Cover/Back Cover Captions

Cover:

A. Mandarin Red vase, Fenton Art Glass Co.

B. Green covered pitcher, Paden City Glass Manufacturing Co.

C. Crystal covered candy jar with amber stain and cut decoration, Westmoreland Glass Co.

D. Opaque white covered candy box, the Beaumont Company.

E. Crystal candlestick with all-over green decoration, gold trim and handpainted floral motif, Lancaster Glass Co.

F. Canary covered candy jar with black decoration and gold floral motif, Fostoria Glass Co.

G. Black sugar and cream (note silver trim) on tray, Central Glass Co.

Back Cover:

H. Amber covered candy jar with cut decoration, Co-Operative Flint Glass Co.

I. Iridescent blue vase with cut decoration, Diamond Glass-Ware Co.

J. Green candleholder with ruffled base, Diamond Glass-Ware Co.

K. Ruby Georgian tumbler, Fenton Art Glass Co.

L. Topaz Iris No. 675 candleholder, H. Northwood Co.

M. Russet No. 705 candlestick, H. Northwood Co.

N. Centerpiece bowl on black base, United States Glass Co.

O. Black lemon tray with Maytime decoration and gold trim, Imperial Glass Co.

All of these are products of the Beaumont Co.
1 and 3. Opaque white No. 115 console bowls
        (note decorations and 2 appropriate base).
4. Opaque white vase on base.

5-7. Crystal candy box (note log finial), crimped bowl and
        large round bowl (note etching and red band decoration).
8 and 10. Opaque white four-footed bowl and plain comport.
9. Satin-finished crystal three-lite candleholder

All of these are products of the Beaumont Co.
11 and **13.** Opaque white No. 148 hexagonal handled trays
(note decorations).
12. Opaque white vase lamp (red bulb inside) on black base.
14-15. Opaque white No. 20 covered candy jars (note
decorations).

16. Opaque white No. 862 ice bucket with multi-color
decoration.
17. Opaque white bowl with platinum band decoration.
18-22. Opaque white salt dip, covered candy jar
(note log finial and decoration), covered candy box,
cornucopia candleholder and comport.

23   24   25   26   27

28   29   30   31   32

33   34   35   36   37   38   39

All of these are products of the Beaumont Co.

23 and **27.** Opaque white vases on bases (note decorations).

24 and **26.** Opaque white fan vases (note decorations).

25. Opaque white No. 148 hexagonal handled tray (note decoration).

28 and **29.** Opaque white vases (note decorations).

30-31. Satin finished crystal tumbler and pitcher (note decoration).

32. Opaque white No. 862 ice bucket (note gold handles and decoration).

33. Opaque white candleholder (note decoration).

34. Opaque white crimped bowl (note decoration).

35-39. Opaque white No. 148 hexagonal cup/saucer, covered candy box, cup/saucer, plate and creamer (note decorations).

51

All of these are products of the Beaumont Co.
40. Opaque white No. 115 console bowl (note decoration).
41. Opaque white fan vase (note decoration).
42. Opaque white bowl (note decoration) on black base.

43-44. Opaque white candleholders and No. 94 console bowl (note decoration).
45. Opaque white comport with gold band decoration.
46-47. Opaque white console bowl and candleholders (note decoration).

All of these are products of the Beaumont Co.

48-50. Opaque white crimped bowl, oval footed bowl and cupped bowl (note decorations).

51-52. Opaque crimped bowl and cornucopia candleholder (note decoration).

53. Opaque white candleholders (note decoration).

54. Opaque white candleholder (note decoration).

55 and 55A. Opaque white bowl with flower frog and covered candy box with log finial (note decoration).

56. Opaque white candleholder (note decoration).

57. Opaque white crimped bowl (note decoration).

58. Opaque white candleholders (note decoration).

59. Opaque white small bowl (note decoration).

60. Opaque white sherbet and tray with owl head handle (note decoration).

61
62
63
64
65
66
67
68
69
70
71
72

Except as indicated for Figs. 65 and 67, these are products of the Beaumont Co.

61-62. Jade green bowl and vases on black bases (note stork decoration).

63. Jade green fluted vase on jade green base.

64. Satin finished green covered comport.

65. United States Glass Co. topaz satin No. 151 candlestick.

66. Crystal candlestick with handpainted floral decoration (note optic pattern inside).

67. Lancaster Glass Co. crystal candlestick with all-over orange decoration and ship motif.

68. Green sandwich tray (note decoration).

69. Jade green covered candy box.

70. Satin finished green No. 137 covered candy box.

71-72. Satin finished green No. 148 hexagonal sugar and creamer.

73

74

75

74

76

76

77

78

79

80

81

All of these are products of the Beaumont Co.
73. Ruby No. 115 console bowl.
74-75. Cobalt blue candleholders and round console bowl.
76. Cobalt blue cornucopia candleholders.
77. Ruby crimped vase (note stork decoration) on black base.

78. Cobalt blue No. 862 ice bucket.
79. Ruby No. 862 ice bucket.
80. Ruby candleholder.
81. Cobalt blue four-footed bowl.

55

All of these are products of the Cambridge Glass Co. (1923–early 1940s), and the color is called "light Emerald" by Cambridge collectors.

82. No. 441 comport

83. No. 300 6" 3-footed candy box.

84. No. 487 cheese comport (goes with 12" oval plate; see Fig. 104).

85. Base for console bowl.

86. No. 410 fan vase.

87. Base to No. 730 candy jar with spiral optic.

88. No. 1917/88 candy jar with optic.

89. Base to No. 300 6" candy box.

90. No. 627 Decagon candlesticks with plate etched decoration.

91. No. 842 Decagon bowl with plate etched decoration.

92. No. 168 sandwich tray with plate etched decoration.

93. No. 627 Decagon candlestick.

94. No. 687 candlestick.

95. Wetherford No. 160 sandwich tray.

All of these are products of the Cambridge Glass Co.
96. Primrose No. 200/2 7" candlesticks.
97. Primrose bowl.
98. Helio No. 101 covered bon bon.
99. Primrose bowl.
100. Ivory No. 1917/361 sandwich tray.

101. Amber No. 735 four-footed oval bowl.
102. Ivory bowl.
103. Mulberry No. 2862 7" candlestick.
104. Amber No. 487 cheese and cracker set.
105. Wetherford No. 145 covered candy jar.
106. Amber No. 168 sandwich tray.

All of these are products of the Cambridge Glass Co.

107. Light Emerald Wetherford No. 154 cheese and cracker.

108. Peach-blo No. 101 covered bon bon.

109. Peach-blo No. 531 comport with deep plate etching.

110. Amber No. 687 candlesticks.

110A. Amber No. 639 candlestick with gold decoration.

111. Amber No. 389 2-pc. relish tray.

112. Amber No. 168 sandwich tray with gold decoration.

113. Peach-blo No. 173 sandwich tray with deep plate etching.

114. Peach-blo No. 103 7" 3-part comport with deep plate etching and gold decoration.

115. Cobalt blue No. 173 sandwich tray with deep plate etching and gold decoration.

116

117

118

117

119

120

119

121

122

123

124

All of these are products of the Central Glass Co. The first item (Fig. 116) is opaque blue glass, but all of the other items are crystal glass.

116. Console bowl with flared and cupped edge.
117. Crystal No. 2000 candlesticks with blue decoration and gold trim.
118. Crystal footed bowl with blue decoration and gold trim.

119. Crystal candlesticks with orange decoration and gold trim.
120. Crystal bowl with orange decoration and gold trim.
121. Crystal No. 1435 pastry (or sandwich) tray with orange decoration and gold trim.
122. Crystal No. 1103 cheese and cracker (note decoration).
123. Crystal Chippendale/Krystol small sugar bowl.
124. Crystal No. 1450 cup and saucer (note etching).

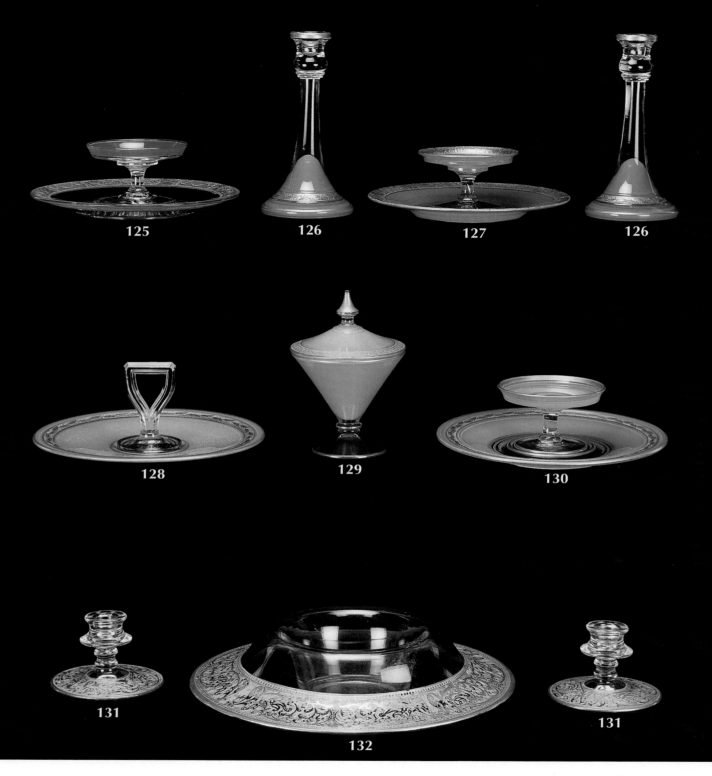

125   **126**   **127**   **126**

128   **129**   **130**

131   **132**   **131**

All of these crystal items are products of the Central Glass Co.

125. Crystal No. 1103 cheese and cracker with blue and gold decoration.

126. Candlesticks with holly motif and orange decoration and gold trim.

127. Crystal No. 1103 cheese and cracker with orange decoration and gold trim

128. Sandwich tray with holly motif and green decoration and gold trim.

129. Covered candy jar with light blue decoration and gold trim.

130. Cheese and cracker with holly motif (plate only) and light blue decoration and gold trim.

131. Crystal No. 2000 candlesticks with heavy gold decoration.

132. Crystal No. 2000 console bowl with heavy gold decoration.

All of these crystal items are products of the Central Glass Co.

133. No. 1435 pastry (or sandwich) tray with orange and gold decoration.

134. Sandwich tray with cut decoration.

135. No. 1435 pastry (or sandwich) tray orange and floral decoration.

136. No. 1435 pastry (or sandwich) tray with cut decoration.

137. No. 1435 pastry (or sandwich) tray with etched decoration and gold trim.

138. No. 1435 pastry (or sandwich) tray with deep plate etching and gold trim.

139. No. 1450 pastry (or sandwich) tray with cut decoration.

140. No. 1435 pastry (or sandwich) tray with cut decoration.

141 **142** **141** **143**

144 **145** **146** **145**

147 **148** **147**

Except for Fig. 143, all of these are products of the Central Glass Co. are opalescent glass.

141. Candlesticks.

142. Console bowl with flared edge.

143. Crystal high footed bon bon with blue and gold decoration.

144. Base for console bowls.

145. Candlesticks.

146. Console bowl with rolled edge.

147. Candlesticks.

148. No. 1435 pastry (or sandwich) tray.

Except as indicated, these are products of the Co-Operative Flint Glass Co.

149. Canary candlestick (two-part mould; Central Glass Co.).

150. Black No. 719 candlestick (two-part mould; made by H. Northwood Co.).

151-152. Cobalt blue 7" candlesticks.

153. Amber No. 481 candlestick.

154. Rose No. 481 candlestick.

155. Amethyst No. 481 candlestick.

156. Decorated crystal No. 431 flower bowl and block with underplate.

157. Sunset rolled edge flower bowl with black base.

158. Midnight Black elephant, no cover (note ruby eyes and decoration with blue jewels).

159. Blue base.

160. Midnight Black base.

161. Sunset base.

162. Midnight Black 9" candlesticks.

163. Midnight Black No. 476 Nubol 12" bowl (shape No. 7) with black base.

All of these are products of the Co-Operative Flint Glass Co.
164. Crystal Adoria sandwich tray with amber stain.
165-167. Adoria covered jelly in crystal with amber stain, amethyst and canary.
168. Canary No. 477 bon bon and cover.
169. Canary candlesticks.

170. Canary bowl with base
171. Amber Ray 9" candlesticks with cut decoration.
172. Amber bowl with cut decoration.
173-174. Crystal Adoria cafe sugar and cafe cream with amber stain.

All of these are products of the Co-Operative Flint Glass Co.

175. Green octagon sandwich tray.

176. Amber No. 520 tall candy jar and cover (note cut decoration).

177. Rose handled bon bon.

178. Crystal handled bon bon with handpainted decoration.

179. Rose covered candy box.

180. Green bowl with black base.

181. Green No. 533 10" handled tray.

182. Crystal Lace Edge handled tray.

183. Crystal No. 60 Lace Edge comport.

184. Crystal Adoria cake tray with cut decoration.

All of these are products of the Davies Glass Manufacturing Co. The footed No. 2 sandwich tray was first advertised in 1924.

185. Crystal sandwich tray with orange/black painted decoration.

186. Amber No. 2 sandwich tray.

187. Opaque red sandwich tray.

188. Amber sandwich tray with leaf motif.

189. Sandwich tray with frosted finish and painted decoration.

190. Crystal No. 2 sandwich tray with cut decoration.

191. Crystal sandwich tray with cut decoration.

192 **193** **194** **193** **195** **196**

197 **198** **199** **198** **200**

201 **202** **203** **204** **205** **206**

All of these are the Diamond Glass-Ware Company's No. 900 line. Introduced in 1925, it is popularly known as Adams Rib today.
192. Green No. 900 vase.
193-194. Blue No. 900 candlesticks and footed bowl (note white trim).
195. Blue iridescent No. 900 mug.
196. Blue iridescent No. 900 pitcher.
197. Marigold iridescent No. 900 fan vase.

198-199. Blue No. 900 candlesticks and footed bowl (note silver trim).
200. Marigold iridescent No. 900 vase or candlestick.
201. Amber No. 900 candlestick.
202. Amber No. 900 plate.
203. Green No. 900 sandwich tray (note decoration).
204. Amber No. 900 cup and saucer.
205. Green No. 900 fan vase.
206. Blue iridescent No. 900 vase or candlestick.

All of these are products of the Diamond Glass-Ware Co. The Victory line was introduced in 1928 (Florence dates it incorrectly as 1929–1932; the factory burned in 1931).

207. Green Victory compote with gold trim.

208. Cobalt blue Victory cup and saucer.

209-210. Pink Victory creamer and mayonnaise set (note gold trim).

211. Pink Victory cheese and cracker set (note gold trim).

212. Amber Victory sugar.

213-214. Green Victory cheese comport and sandwich tray (note gold trim).

215. Blue candlestick (note gold/black decoration).

216-217. Green and pink (note floral decoration) relish trays; this design was patented in 1927.

218. Green candlestick with crimped base.

All of these are products of the Diamond Glass-Ware Co.
219. Black vase with "hammered gold" treatment (c. 1924).
220. Black candlestick with gold decoration.
221. Black cheese and cracker set with gold and floral decoration.
222-223. Black candlesticks and sandwich tray with "hammered gold" decoration.

224. Crystal sandwich tray with black/gold decoration.
225. Black No. 99 candlestick with silver Jack and the Bean Stalk decoration, c. 1930.
226. Crystal cheese and cracker set with orange/black decoration and gold trim.

227   228   229   230

231

232   234

232   233   234

All of these are products of the Dunbar Glass Corporation.
227-228. Vases with lustre treatment.
229. Pitcher from No. 5024 ice tea set (note faint lustre treatment).
230. Pink covered pitcher and four tumblers.

231. Lustre pitcher and six tumblers.
232. Amber candlesticks (note cut decoration).
233. Amber rolled edge console bowl.
234. Amber candlesticks.

235   236   237   238   239

240   241   242

243   244   245

All of these are products of the Dunbar Glass Corporation.
235. Crystal hifoot covered comport with all-over white, floral motif decoration and silver trim.
236. Satin finished crystal covered candy jar with decoration.
237-238. Crystal hifoot covered comports with floral decorations.
239. Amber covered candy jar with cut decoration.
240. Pink cheese and cracker set with cut decoration.

241. Green cheese and cracker set with gold decoration.
242. Pink cheese and cracker set.
243. Satin finished pink cheese and cracker set with floral decoration.
244. Pink sandwich tray with floral decoration.
245. Pink covered candy box with cut decoration and black trim.

All of these are products of the Dunbar Glass Corporation.

246. Crystal covered candy jar with red lustre (this was sometimes called a "bonbonierre").

247. Pink fan vase.

248. No. 3063 pink bridge set (No. 1247 Servette with four tumblers; note clubs, diamonds, hearts and spades decoration).

249. Blue lustre pitcher and six tumblers.

250. Ruby pitcher and five tumblers; note traces of silver trim (this was called a "tomato juice set" in 1935).

251. Satin finished green base for covered candy jar.

252. Pink sandwich tray with cut decoration.

253. Crystal covered candy jar with all-over yellow decoration and black trim.

254. Pink candlestick with gold decoration.

255   256   257   258   259

260   262   261   263

264   265   266   267

All of these are products of the Duncan-Miller Glass Co.
255. Ruby Canterbury No. 115-112 flower arranger.
256. Green No. 12 9" vase with crimped top.
257. Ruby No. 103 Georgian tumbler.
258-259. Ruby and blue No. 103 Georgian tumblers and pitcher
260. Amber No. 103 Georgian plate.
261. Pink No. 38 bowl.

262. Green No. 91 cheese comport (note gold trim).
263. Ruby No. 26 lunch plate or sandwich tray
264. Green No. 38 lunch plate or sandwich tray with cut decoration.
265. Lustre No. 908 flower bowl on matching base (also called foot)
266. Lustre base or foot.
267. Lustre base or foot.

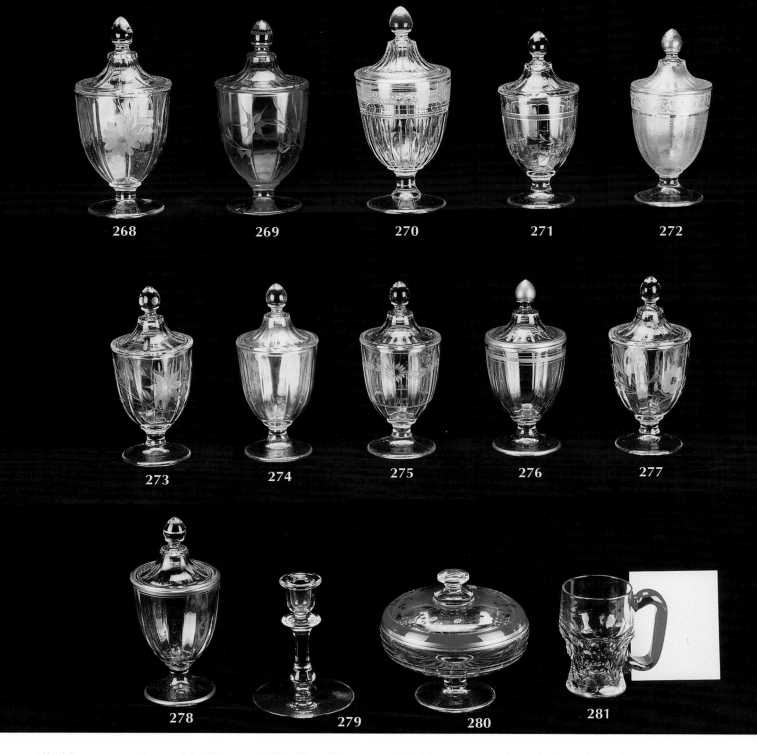

268 269 270 271 272

273 274 275 276 277

278 279 280 281

All of these are products of the Duncan-Miller Glass Co. Fig. 269 is blue glass, and the rest are crystal glass. Some of the No. 25 candy jars may show a rib optic pattern inside.

268. No. 25 covered candy jar with cut decoration.
269. Blue No. 25 covered candy jar with cut decoration.
270. No. 95 covered candy jar with decoration.
271. No. 25 covered candy jar with cut decoration and painted trim.
272. No. 25 covered candy jar with all-over texture (except foot) and gold decoration.

273. No. 25 covered candy jar with cut decoration.
274. No. 25 covered candy jar with lustre decoration.
275. No. 25 covered candy jar with cut decoration.
276. No. 25 covered candy jar with gold decoration.
277. No. 25 covered candy jar with cut decoration.
278. No. 25 covered candy jar with gold decoration.
279. No. 28 6" candlestick.
280. No. 95 covered sweetmeat (note decoration).
281. No. 103 Georgian tumbler with applied ruby handle.

282   283   284

285   286   287

288   289   290

Except as indicated, these are products of the Duncan-Miller Glass Co.

282. Crystal No. 38 lunch plate or sandwich tray with cut decoration (note flat top of the handle; compare with others in this row).

283. Crystal sandwich tray with cut decoration and black decorated handle (made by Westmoreland Glass Co.).

284. Pink sandwich tray with cut decoration (made by Liberty Works).

285. Crystal No. 26 lunch plate or sandwich tray with decoration.

286. Crystal No. 38 lunch plate or sandwich tray with cut decoration.

287. Pink No. 38 lunch plate or sandwich tray with cut decoration.

288. Pink No. 99 lunch plate or sandwich tray (note decoration).

289. Pink No. 38 lunch plate with gold trim.

290. Crystal No. 99 lunch plate or sandwich tray.

291   292   293   294   295

296   297   298   299   300

301   302   303   304   305   306   307

Among the products of the Economy Glass Co. was the pattern called "Round Robin" in several books on Depression Era glass. Except for Figs. 294, 295 and 306, the items shown are Economy's No. 1500 (Round Robin) line.

291. Crystal No. 1500 (Round Robin) flat foot vase (note decoration).

292. Crystal No. 1500 (Round Robin) mayonnaise bowl (note decoration).

293. Crystal No. 1500 (Round Robin) covered candy jar with all-over yellow decoration and black trim.

294. Crystal and Aqua Marine No. 16 covered bon bon, c. 1928.

295. Crystal and Rose Marie No. 14 covered bowl, c. 1928.

296. Green No. 1500 (Round Robin) plate.

297. Green No. 1500 (Round Robin) saucer and cup.

298-299. Green No. 1500 (Round Robin) sugar and cream.

300. Green No. 1500 (Round Robin) mayonnaise bowl with deep plate etching.

301-302. Iridescent No. 1500 (Round Robin) cream and sugar.

303. Iridescent No. 1500 (Round Robin) sherbet.

304. Light amber No. 1500 (Round Robin) mayonnaise bowl.

305. Pink cover for No. 1500 (Round Robin) candy jar.

306. Crystal tumbler with cut decoration.

307. Pink No. 1500 (Round Robin) low footed comport.

308   309   310   311

312   313   314   315   316   317   318

319   320

321   322   323   324   325   326

All of these are products of the Fenton Art Glass Co.
308. Chinese Yellow No. 894 vase with unusual decoration.
309. Black No. 649 10" candlestick.
310. Chinese Yellow No. 604 12" flared and cupped bowl with black base.
311. Mandarin Red No. 888 10" vase.
312. Lilac No. 1608 Dolphin deep oval bowl.

313-318. Jade Green No. 1611 Georgian (originally called Agua Caliente) cupped sherbet, whiskey, orange juice, table tumbler, ice tea and pitcher.
319. Ruby No. 1611 Georgian table tumbler, c. 1930s.
320. Ruby Georgian table tumbler, c. 1950s (note larger size).
321-326. No. 549 8¹/₂" candlesticks in Jade Green, Moonstone (black foot), Pekin Blue (gold trim), Jade Green (Moonstone foot), Flame (blue foot), and Celeste Blue.

327   328   329   330   329

331   332   333   334

335   336   337   338   338

All of these iridescent Wisteria (sometimes spelled "Wistaria") pieces are products of the Fenton Art Glass Co.
327. No. 1006 salad plate.
328. No. 103 sherbet.
329. No. 349 10" candlesticks.
330. No. 604 12" flared and cupped bowl with black base.
331. Fan vase made from No. 735 candy jar base.

332. No. 550 aquarium.
333. No. 643 covered bon bon.
334. No. 6121 6½" flared vase on black base.
335. No. 9 covered candy jar.
336. No. 643 salver compote.
337. Fan vase made from No. 736 candy jar base.
338. No. 316 candleholders.

All of these are products of the Fenton Art Glass Co.
339. Jade green No. 2007 cupped bowl with black base.
340. Ruby No. 643 plate compote.
341. Celeste Blue No. 349 10" candlesticks.
342. Black (note decoration) No. 606 bowl with black base.
343. Black No. 848 square-shaped bowl with black base.
344. Grecian Gold No. 570 fan vase.
345-346. Velva Rose No. 3 sugar and cream.
347. Royal Blue No. 1611 Georgian candlestick.
348. Florentine Green No. 316 candlestick.

349. Topaz bobeche.
350. Ruby No. 640 cupped bowl.
351-352. Ruby No. 1639 sugar and cream.
353. Florentine Green No. 643 covered bon bon.
354. Velva Rose No. 317 candlestick.
355. Topaz No. 923 mayonnaise.
356. Green No. 1503-A Dolphin flared bowl.
357. Crystal No. 2100 Viking Boat with gold decoration (signed by Louise Piper).

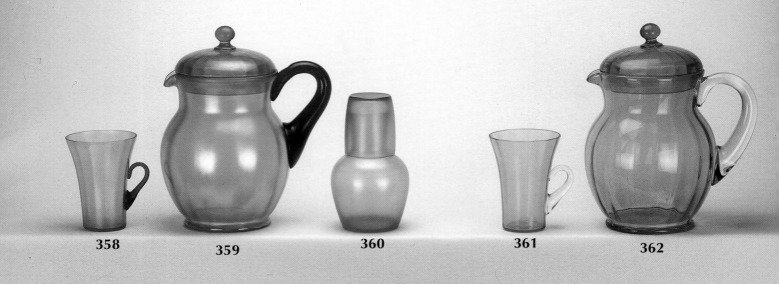

358   359   360   361   362

363   364   365

366   367   368   367

358-359. Fenton Celeste Blue No. 220 handled tumbler and covered pitcher.

360. Fenton Celeste Blue No. 401 night set.

361-362. Fry Royal Blue No. 8711 handled tumbler ("Fry Quality" mark) and Royal Blue No. 11 covered pitcher.

363. Fry No. 19814 Rose sandwich tray with black/gold decoration.

364. Fry No. 19814 black sandwich tray.

365. Fry No. 19814 Rose sandwich tray with satin finished handle and etched decoration.

366. Fry amber candlestick with gold trim (note original paper label).

367-368. Fry Rose candlesticks with black/gold decoration and Fry Rose console bowl (these pieces comprised the No. 25002 console set).

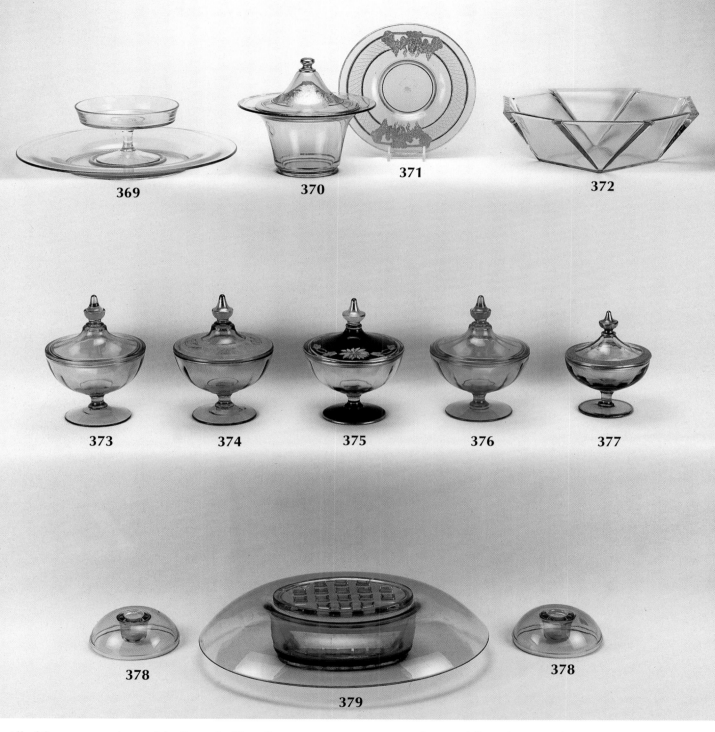

All of these are products of the Fostoria Glass Co.

369. Azure No. 2368 cheese and cracker set.

370-371. Orchid No. 2380 confection and cover with matching plate (note decoration).

372. Amber No. 2402 bowl.

373-376. Green, amber (gold decorated pheasant motif by the Wheeling Decorating Co.), canary (note decoration) and blue No. 2250 covered

candy jars (¹/₂ lb.). These candy jars are similar to some made at Paden City, but Fostoria's have mould marks which go entirely up the finial on the cover.

377. Orchid No. 2250 covered candy jar (¹/₄ lb.).

378. Orchid No. 2372 candle blocks.

379. Orchid No. 2371 centerpiece with No. 2371 flower holder.

All of these are products of the Fostoria Glass Co.
380. Ebony No. 2288 Tut vase.
381. Green No. 2219 covered candy jar.
382. No. 1630 Alexis sweet pea vase with dark brown all-over painted decoration.
383. Green No. 2275 candlestick.
384. Green No. 2275 candlestick.
385. Ebony No. 2297 candlestick.
386. Blue No. 2562 candlestick.
387-389. Azure, blue and green No. 2368 footed cheese comports.

390. Green No. 2324 candlestick.
391. Amber No. 2324 candlesticks.
392. Green three-toed bowl with gold trim (note the unusually-shaped feet).
393. Amber No. 2447 duo candlestick.
394. Orchid No. 2331 candy box and cover.
395. Ebony base.
396. Ebony base.
397. Green No. 2267 console bowl.

All of these are products of the Fostoria Glass Co.

398. Crystal No. 2219 covered candy jar with orange decoration and gold trim.

399. Crystal No. 2219 covered candy jar with gold trim.

400. Crystal No. 2327 comport with cutting and orange decoration.

401. Crystal No. 2219 covered candy jar with cut decoration.

402. Crystal No. 2327 comport with all-over yellow/orange decoration.

403. Crystal No. 2496 Baroque 5½" candlestick.

404. Mother of Pearl lustre No. 2250 covered candy jar (¼ lb.)

405. Mother of Pearl lustre No. 2250 covered candy jar (1 lb.).

406. Crystal No. 2368 footed cheese comport with gold decoration.

407. Crystal No. 2056 American jelly and cover.

408. Crystal No. 2375 candlesticks with gold decoration.

409. Crystal No. 2375 bowl with gold decoration.

410. Crystal No. 2496 Baroque 4" candlestick.

All of these are products of the Hazel-Atlas Glass Co.
411. Black Ovide sherbet with "cloverleaf" decoration.
412-413. Crystal Ovide sugar and cream with all-over
    yellow decoration.
414-415. Black Ovide sugar and cream (note silver
    decoration).
416. Black Ovide plate (note silver decoration).
417. Black Ovide cup and saucer (note silver decoration).

418. Black No. 3025 bowl.
419. Black bowl.
420. Green No. 3027 pitcher.
421. Green covered candy jar.
422. Yellow stained covered candy jar with black trim.
423. Yellow stained comport with black trim.
424. Black Ovide covered candy jar.
425-428. Georgian tumblers in light blue, light amber, dark
    amber and dark blue.

Except as indicated, all of these are products of A. H. Heisey and Co.

429. Crystal covered comport, made in two-part mould (note decoration).

430. Velva Rose covered comport by Fenton Art Glass (made in four-part mould).

431. Flamingo octagonal foot (see Fig. 439).

432. Moon Gleam No. 106 candlestick.

433. Flamingo No. 126 candlestick.

434. Crystal covered comport (note decoration).

435. Flamingo two-handled bon bon.

436. Crystal sandwich tray (note decoration); the loop-shaped handle is similar to those made by Beaumont, Duncan Miller and Fenton).

437. Crystal No. 411 Tudor covered lemon dish (note iridescent treatment).

438. Crystal No. 465 covered candy jar with blue and gold decoration (note optic).

439. Flamingo No. 1231 bowl (octagonal base fits into matching foot).

440. Crystal overed candy jar with blue and gold decoration.

All of these are products of A. H. Heisey and Co.

441. Crystal No. 1506 Whirlpool tumbler.
442. Crystal Georgian-style goblet.
443-444. Crystal No. 1170 hotel sugar and cream (gold decoration).
445. Crystal No. 465 covered candy jar.
446. Crystal base for plain candy jar (light iridescent treatment).
447. Crystal No. 1428 Warwick horn of plenty vase.
448. Crystal mayonnaise set.

449. Crystal covered sugar bowl.
450-451. Crystal No. 355 hotel cream and hotel sugar.
452. Crystal No. 353 individual almond.
453. Crystal No. 353 individual almond (satin finish and gold trim).
454. Crystal sandwich tray (note loop-shaped handle, similar to those made by Beaumont, Duncan-Miller and Fenton).
455. Crystal No. 473 sugar cubes and cream set (gold decoration).
456. Crystal sandwich tray, cut decoration (note shape of handle).

All of these are products of the Hocking Glass Co.

457-458. Green and crystal No. 2657 Colonial pattern milk pitchers (called Knife and Fork by some collectors).

459-460. Opaque white Sandwich punch cups and punch bowl on base.

461. Satin finished crystal round covered candy box with painted decoration.

462. Crystal No. 1093 covered candy jar.

463. Crystal No. 1093 covered candy jar with orange decoration and gold trim.

464. Crystal No. 1093 covered candy jar with green decoration.

465. Crystal Manhattan candlestick.

466. Queen Mary footed comport.

467. Crystal No. 1300 sandwich tray (note traces of red decoration).

All of these are products of the Hocking Glass Co.
468. Green No. 1093 covered candy jar.
469-470. Forest Green punch cups and punch bowl on base (this set was made in Royal Ruby in the 1930s).
471. Pink No. 906 Old Colony (Lace Edge) covered bowl.

472. Green Spiral sandwich tray.
473. Green satin finished Spiral covered candy box.
474. Green Spiral covered candy box.
475. Green No. 906 Old Colony (Lace Edge) bowl.
476. Pink No. 906 Old Colony (Lace Edge) sandwich tray.

Original color ad for the Hocking Glass Company's 1300/15 set (now called Rings or Banded Rings by collectors).

477   478   479   480   481   482

483   484   485   486   485

487
488   489   490   491   492

All of these are products of Imperial Glass.
477. Amethyst No. 635 candlestick.
478. Saphire No. 600 candlestick.
479. Ruby No. 694 wide vase.
480. Rubigold No. 300 basket.
481. Amethyst No. 419 candlestick.
482. Green No. 70 vase.
483. Satin finished No. 169 mayonnaise set with unusual decoration.

484. Green cigarette holder.
485. Crystal No. 637 candleholders (with blue/white painted decoration).
486. Crystal crimped console bowl (with blue/white painted decoration).
487-488. Ruby sugar and cream.
489. Rubigold No. 600 cupped bowl.
490. Ruby No. 711 comport and No. 725 underplate.
491. Ruby No. 711 Caliente tumbler.
492. Green No. 717 covered candy box with gold trim.

All of these are products of Imperial Glass.
493. Rose Pink No. 169 mayonnaise set (note decoration).
494. Iris Ice No. 300 basket.
495. Blue Ice No. 514 bowl.
496. Peacock iridescent No. 514 bowl (collectors call this "smoke").
497. Green No. 725 mint tray with cut decoration.
498. Golden Green No. 600 covered comport.
499. Pink No. 725 bon bon tray with decal decoration.
500. Rose Pink No. 717 covered candy box.

501. Green No. 725 bon bon tray with gold trim.
502. Amber No. 600 covered bon bon.
503. Crystal No. 724/2 covered dish with decal decoration.
504. Iris Ice No. 725 sandwich tray.
505. Blue Ice rolled edge comport.
506. Green No. 724/2 covered dish.
507. Rubigold (marigold iridescence on crystal) No. 664 sandwich tray with black decoration.
508. Rose Ice rolled edge comport.

All of these Cape Cod items are products of Imperial Glass.
509. 160/163 ruby 30 oz. decanter and stopper.
510. 160/163 Ritz Blue 30 oz. decanter and stopper.
511. 160 Ritz Blue wine.
512. 160/37 Ritz Blue saucer.
513. 160/3D Ritz Blue 7" salad plate.
514. 160 ruby wine.
515. 160/5D ruby plate.
516. 160 Ritz Blue juice tumbler.

517. 160/37 Ritz Blue coffee cup.
518. 160 Ritz Blue iced tea tumbler.
519. 160 Ritz Blue sherbet.
520. 160/1W Ritz Blue fruit bowl.
521. 160/37 ruby coffee cup.
522. 160 ruby sherbet.
523. 160 ruby juice tumbler.
524. 160 ruby cocktail.
525. 160/37 ruby saucer.
526. 160 ruby goblet.

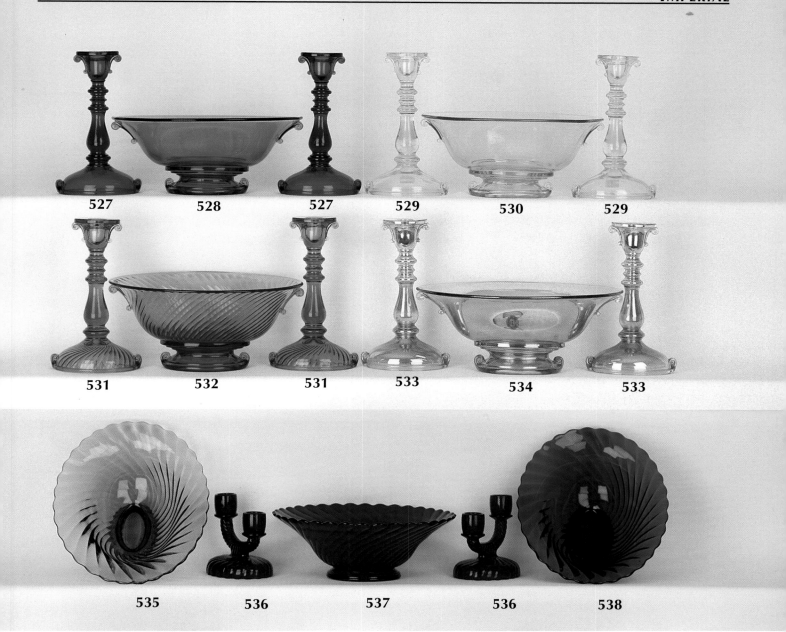

527   528   527   529   530   529

531   532   531   533   534   533

535   536   537   536   538

These console sets were made by Imperial. Items from the No. 320 line were combined (the swirl optic was re-numbered No. 313; Weatherman called all of these "Packard," and did not differentiate between plain and optic). Carnival collectors refer to No. 320 as Double Scroll.
527. Blue No. 320 oval 8¼" candlesticks.
528. Blue No. 320 10½" oval bowl.
529. Golden Green No. 320 oval 8¼" candlesticks.
530. Golden Green No. 320 10½" oval bowl.
531. Green No. 313 oval candlestick (swirl optic).

532. Green No. 313 10½" oval bowl (swirl optic).
533. Rubigold No. 320 oval candlestick.
534. Rubigold No. 320 10½" oval bowl.
Imperial's No. 153 twin candlesticks were combined with round or oval bowls to form console sets in many different colors.
535. Amber No. 153 oval bowl.
536. Ritz Blue No. 153 twin candlesticks.
537. Ritz Blue No. 153B round bowl.
538. Stiegel Green No. 153 oval bowl.

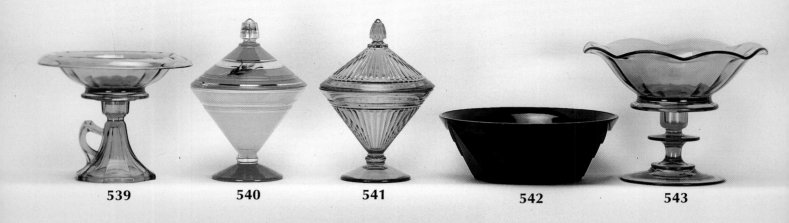

539   540   541   542   543

544   545   546   547

548   549   550   551

All of these are products of the Indiana Glass Co.

539. Amber handled candlestick with peg bowl (two separate pieces).

540. Crystal covered candy jar with orange/white decoration, handpainting and silver trim.

541. Amber covered candy jar (note rib optic).

542. Black No. 610 8½" bowl.

543. Amber candlestick with crimped peg bowl (two separate pieces).

544. Amber three-toed bowl (note rib optic).

545. Ruby No. 300-1/2 footed bowl.

546. No. 9 handled butter ball with ruby stain and cut decoration.

547. No. 604 footed bon bon and cover with ruby stain.

548. Pink covered candy box with octagonal cover (note decoration).

549. Crystal No. 9 ruby-stained covered relish (note decoration).

550. Pink covered candy box (note decoration)

551. Crystal coasters with all-over orange decoration.

552   553   554   553   555

556   557   556   558   559

560   561   562   563   564

All of these are products of the Indiana Glass Co.

552. Green sandwich tray with black decoration and gold trim.

553. Crystal candlesticks with orange decoration and handpainted floral motif.

554. Large console bowl with orange decoration and handpainted floral motif.

555. Crystal No. 232 relish with all-over red-orange decoration.

556. Crystal candlesticks with all-over orange decoration.

557. Crystal bowl with all-over orange decoration on black glass base.

558. Amber Lace Edge bowl.

559. No. 9 bowl with all-over canary decoration.

560. No. 603 candlestick (note decoration).

561. No. 603 candlestick (note decoration).

562. Black (satin-finished) candlestick.

563. Crystal candlestick with gold trim.

564. Black candlestick.

565   566   565   567   568   569   568

570   571   572   573

574   575   576

All of these crystal glass items with all-over painted decoration (and black trim) are products of the Indiana Glass Co.

565. Candlesticks with all-over blue decoration (from No. 4 Console Set).

566. Bowl with all-over blue decoration.

567. Candlestick with all-over canary decoration (from No. 4 Console Set).

568. Candlesticks with all-over orange decoration (from No. 4 Console Set).

569. Footed bowl with all-over orange decoration.

570. Footed bowl with all-over orange decoration.

571. Vase with all-over jade green decoration.

572. Candy jar base with all-over orange decoration.

573. Sandwich tray with all-over canary decoration.

574. Bowl with all-over jade green decoration on black glass base (extra base shown for detail).

575. Sandwich tray with all-over orange decoration.

576. Bowl ("B" shape from No. 4 Console Set) with all-over orange decoration on black glass base.

577   578   579   580

581   582   583

584   585   586   587

All of these are products of the Jeannette Glass Co.

577 and **580.** Iridescent crepe effect covered candy jars.

578. Iridescent crepe effect pitcher with cover.

579. Iridescent No. 21 crepe effect vase.

581. Iridescent footed bowl (from 26-97 buffet set or 27-49 console set).

582. Blue No. 5215 bowl (note integral foot).

583. Iridescent No. 5178 footed bowl.

584. Amber cream.

585-587. Iridescent No. 132 (also No. 5108) covered candy jars.

All of these are products of the Jeannette Glass Co.

588. Iridescent Anniversary plate with crimped edge.

589. Crystal Anniversary 12½" sandwich plate.

590. Amber iridescent No. X-33 Ringed Design covered candy jar.

591. Crystal sandwich tray (note decoration).

592. Amber candlestick (from X-68 buffet set).

593. Iridescent covered kitchen container.

594. Green No. 5180 sandwich tray (note decoration) and gold trim.

595. Decorated bowl from X-31 console set.

596. Decorated No. 5215 bowl on black base.

597   597   598   599   598   600

601   602   603

604   605   606

All of these are products of the Jeannette Glass Co.

597. Iridescent No. 5201 candlesticks.

598. No. 5132 hexagon style candlesticks with all-over orange decoration and black trim.

599. No. 5164 bowl with all-over orange decoration and black trim.

600. No. 5625 amber iridescent auto vase.

601. Iridescent sandwich tray with cut decoration, c. 1925.

602. Iridescent sandwich tray, c. 1925.

603. Iridescent No. 5180 sandwich tray.

604. Iridescent bowl.

605. Iridescent No. 2100 three-piece nesting ash tray set.

606. Iridescent No. 5186 bowl and black base.

All of these are products of the Jeannette Glass Co.
607. Iridescent No. 5179 candlesticks.
608. Iridescent rolled edge bowl (from X-68 buffet set).
609. Iridescent footed bowl.
610. Iridescent No. 5164 bowl on black base.
611. Iridescent No. 88 rolled edge nappy on black base.

612. Iridescent No. 5178 footed bowl.
613-615. These footed bowls (blue iridescent, dark amethyst iridescent and green iridescent, respectively) were made from the standard footed bowl shown with Jeannette's X-68 buffet set or No. 26-49 console set.

All of these green items are products of the D. C. Jenkins Glass Co.

616-618. No. 250 pitcher, tumbler and salad plate.
619. No. 8-1/2 pitcher.
620. Kerosene lamp.
621-625. No. 250 vase, goblet, 4½" nappy, wine, and footed jelly and cover.

626. No. 570 covered water jug, refrigerator style.
627. No. 190C berry dish.
628-634. No. 190 footed soda, cup and saucer, berry nappy, salad plate, tall sundae, footed soda and low sundae.

All of these crystal items are products of the D. C. Jenkins
Glass Co.
635. No. 77 covered candy jar.
636. Covered comport.
637-638. Tumbler and pitcher.
639. Tumbler.

640. Covered pitcher.
641-642. No. 202 tumbler and pitcher.
643. Satin finished lamp.
644-647. No. 202 spooner, cream, covered sugar and tall
celery.

648   649   650   651

652   653   654   655

656   657   659   661   663
656   658   660   662

These are products of the D. C. Jenkins Glass Co. (except for Figs. 649, 655 and 657, all have an iridescent finish, usually marigold; Figs. 649 and 655 have a distinct heavy texture).

648. No. 312 vase.
649. No. 310 vase with heavy applied red decoration on crystal glass.
650. No. 50 salad plate.
651. No. 75 saucer.
652. No. 400 bowl.
653. Bowl.

654. No. 202 8" flared nappy.
655. Covered comport with heavy applied blue decoration and floral motif.
656. No. 336 casserole and cover.
657. Satin finished pink No. 560 covered nappy.
658. No. 636 nappy.
659. No. 460 swan.
660. No. 112 ashtray.
661. No. 17 wine.
662. No. 400 covered nappy.
663. No. 400 cream.

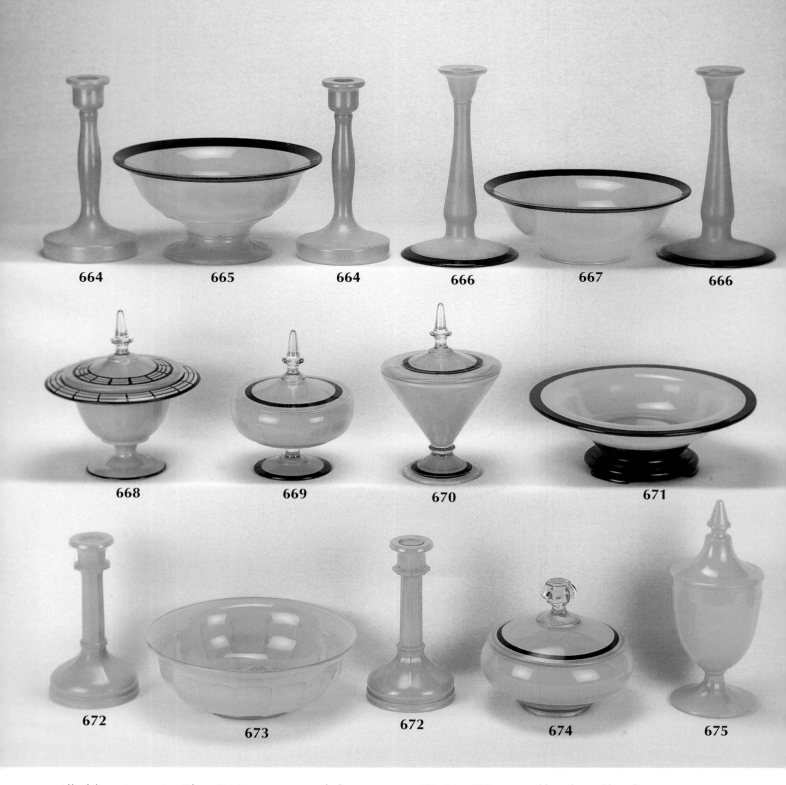

664   665   664   666   667   666

668   669   670   671

672   673   672   674   675

All of these Lancaster Glass Co. items are crystal glass which has been decorated with yellow paint and often accented with black.

664. No. 984 candlesticks.
665. No. 85 flared bowl.
666. No. 85 candlesticks.
667. No. 81 orange bowl.
668. No. 906 covered candy jar.

669. No. 788 covered low footed bon bon.
670. No. 83 covered candy jar.
671. No. 984 flared nappy on black base.
672. No. 85 candlesticks.
673. No. 81 orange bowl.
674. No. 788 covered candy box.
675. No. 627 covered candy jar.

676

677

678

679

680

681

682

683

684

685

686

685

687

Except as indicated, these are products of the Lancaster Glass Co.
676. Iridescent No. 85 6" plate.
677. Black No. 620 11" bowl.
678. Iridescent No. 85 8" plate.
679. Pink satin finished No. R1660 plate.
680. Green No. 98D footed comport.
681-682. Amber (note decoration) and black covered candy boxes (made by the Fostoria Glass Company

and the Central Glass Company, respectively; Lancaster made a similar item).
683. Pink satin finished No. 605 comport.
684 and **687.** No. A1-1/2 vases.
685. Pink No. 615 candlesticks.
686. No. 788 covered bon bon.

688

689

690

691

692

693

694

695

696

697

698

699

700

All of these are products of the Lancaster Glass Co.

688-689. Iridescent fan vase made from base for No. 83 covered candy jar and iridescent base for No. 83 covered candy jar.

690. Green 6½" cupped bowl with external "crackle" pattern.

691. Iridescent No. 86 comport.

692. Iridescent bowl.

693. Iridescent No. 86 rolled edge bowl on black base.

694. Iridescent No. 427 wall vase.

695. Iridescent fan vase made from No. 83 candy jar base (note optic).

696-697. Iridescent No. 75 cream and sugar with cut decoration.

698. Amber vase with deep rolled edge.

699. Iridescent No. 88 lily bowl.

700. Olive green No. 98 bon bon base.

All of these are products of the Lancaster Glass Co.
701-702. Crystal (note decoration) and amber No. 83 covered
   candy jars
703 and **705.** No. 88 high footed covered candy jars (note
   decorations).
704. Green No. 854 candlesticks (note decoration).

706. No. 85 flared comport (note decoration).
707. No. 85 rolled edge comport (note decoration).
708. No. 85 flared comport (note decoration).
709. Iridescent No. 81 orange bowl.
710. No. 984 flared nappy on black base.
711. Iridescent No. 86 high footed flared bon bon.

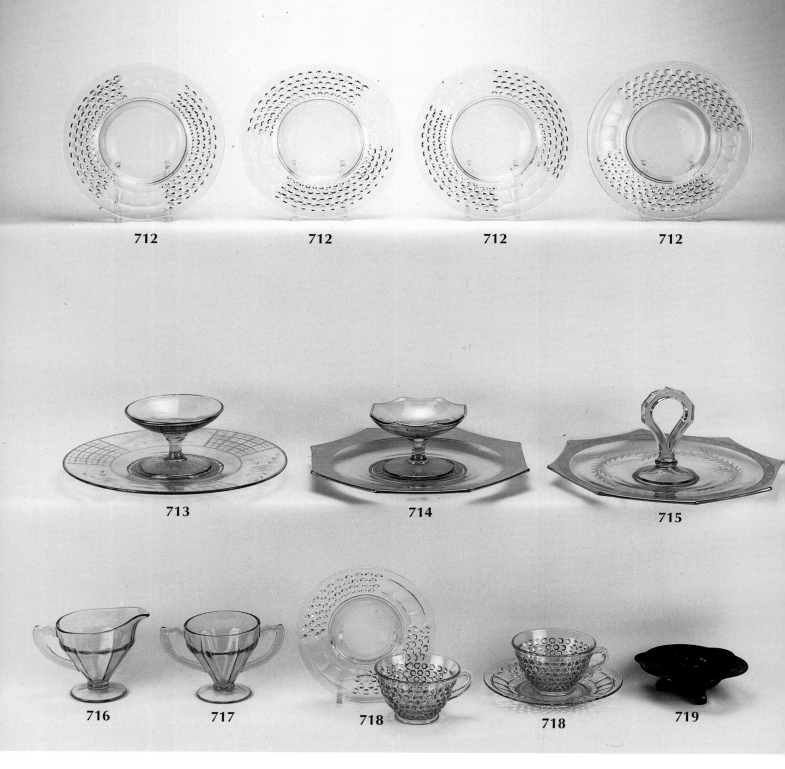

712   712   712   712

713   714   715

716   717   718   718   719

All of these are products of the Liberty Works.
712. Pink American Pioneer plates.
713. Pink cheese and cracker set (note decoration).
714. Green Octagon cheese and cracker set.

715. Pink Octagon Optic sandwich tray.
716-717. Pink cream and sugar.
718. Pink American Pioneer cup and saucer sets.
719. Black candlestick.

720   721   722   723   724   725

726   727   728   729

730   731   732

All of these are products of the McKee Glass Co.
720. Amber No. 2 covered comport.
721. Rose Pink No. 4 covered candy jar.
722. Green No. 4 covered candy jar with black trim.
723. Crystal No. 100 covered candy jar with decoration and gold trim.
724. Green No. 156 Octagon Edge covered candy jar.
725. Rose Pink No. 2 covered comport.
726. Rose Pink No. 152 covered candy box with cut decoration.

727. Green No. 156 Octagon Edge covered candy box.
728. Rose Pink covered candy box with cut decoration.
729. Pink No. 156 Octagon Edge covered candy box.
730. Jade green No. 156 Octagon Edge sandwich tray.
731. Amber No. 151 handled nut bowl.
732. Green No. 151 lunch plate or sandwich tray with black decoration and gold trim.

All of these are products of the McKee Glass Co.

733. Crystal No. 100 covered candy jar with painted decoration and trim.

734. Crystal No. 90 covered candy jar (¹/₂ lb.) with painted decoration and trim.

735. Amber No. 100 covered candy jar.

736. Apple green Two Panel covered sugar bowl.

737. Rose Pink No. 2 covered comport (note optic).

738. Green No. 4 covered candy jar with cut decoration and gold trim (note optic).

739. Amber No. 2 covered comport (note optic).

740. Rose Pink No. 156 Optic, Octagon Edge, sandwich tray.

741. Amber square covered candy jar with Brocade pattern decoration.

742. Green No. 100 candlestick.

743. Crystal No. 4 candy jar base with rolled edge (note orange decoration and black trim).

744. Topaz No. 151 lunch plate or sandwich tray.

745. Green covered butter dish.

746. Crystal No. 4 candy jar base with rolled edge (note blue decoration and black trim).

747. Rose Pink small No. 156 Optic, Octagon Edge, comport.

748

749

750

751

752

753

754

The sandwich trays in the top row were made by the Bartlett-Collins Glass Co. The items in the middle and bottom rows were made by the New Cumberland Glass Co.

748. Crystal No. 87 sandwich tray with all-over blue decoration and black trim.

749. Green No. 87 sandwich tray with handpainted decoration.

750. Crystal No. 87 sandwich tray with all-over green decoration and decorated black handle.

751. Crystal covered comport and underplate with all-over painted decoration.

752. Crystal sandwich tray with all-over painted decoration.

753. Light green sandwich tray with cut decoration.

754. Satin finished crystal covered comport with painted decoration and trim.

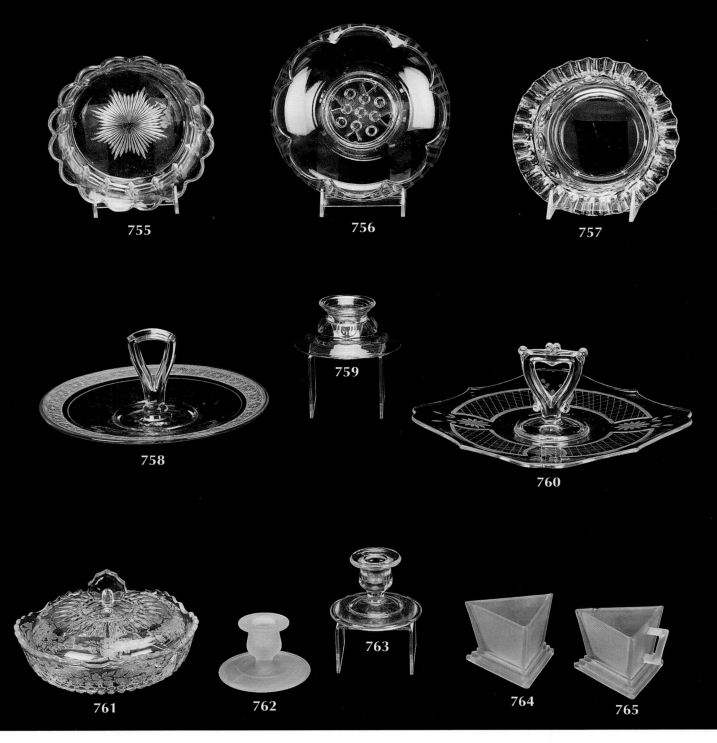

755

756

757

758

759

760

761

762

763

764

765

All of these are products of the New Martinsville Glass Co.
755. Crystal No. 626 bowl.
756. Pink bowl with integral flower frog, c. 1926 (note cut decoration; see also Fig. 787).
757. Crystal No. 37 (Moondrops) bowl with crimped edge.
758. Pink No. 10 sandwich tray with gold decoration.
759. Crystal no. 37 (Moondrops) candlestick.

760. Crystal No. 35 sandwich tray with cut decoration.
761. No. 42 Radiance covered candy box with deep plate etching.
762-763. Jade Green and green No. 10/4 candlesticks.
764-765. Green satin finished No. 33 Modernistic sugar and cream.

766

767

768

769

770

771

772

773

774

Except as indicated, these are products of the New Martinsville Glass Co.

766. Crystal No. 4527 Janice flared vase with deep plate etching.

767. Paden City No. 533 sandwich tray with deep plate etching.

768. Crystal No. 42 Radiance sandwich tray with deep plate etching.

769. Paden City Crystal No. 555 sandwich tray with deep plate etching.

770. Green sandwich tray.

771. Crystal No. 37 (Moondrops) three-section relish dish.

772. Crystal covered candy box with deep plate etching.

773. Crystal No. 10 three-section covered candy box with gold decoration.

774. Crystal covered candy box with etched decoration.

Except as indicated, these are products of the New Martinsville Glass Co.

775. Black No. 42 Radiance 12" crimped vase.

776. Amber No. 42 Radiance handled tray.

777. Pink Wise Owl pitcher.

778. Ruby No. 42 Radiance cupped bowl.

779. Dark blue covered candy box made by Viking in the 1940s–1950s.

780. Blue No. 10-12 Princess console bowl on black base.

781. Pink No. 37 (Moondrops) crimped bowl.

782. Green No. 10 sandwich tray with cut decoration.

783. Green No. 35 handled tray.

784. Satin finished green No. 10/4 candlestick.

785. Green sandwich tray with deep plate etching and gold decoration.

786. Green no. 10-2 Queen Anne box (note handpainted decoration) for dresser set.

787. Pink bowl with integral flower frog, c. 1926 (note cut decoration; see also Fig. 756).

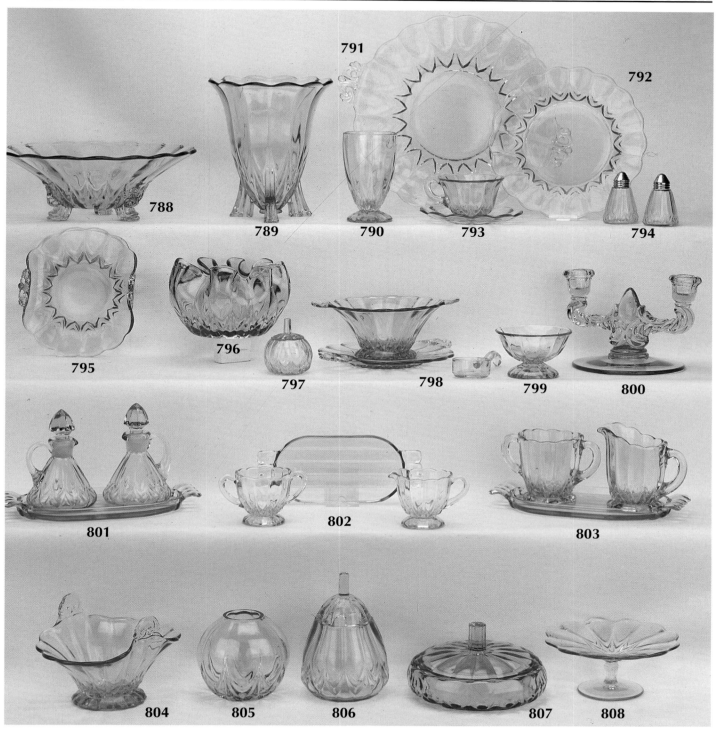

All of these are products of the New Martinsville Glass Co. Except for Fig. 800, these items in pale blue are from New Martinsville's No. 45 (or 4500) Janice line. Original item numbers are given from company catalogues.

788. No. 4511 flared footed bowl.
789. No. 4527 8" flared vase.
790. No. 4581 luncheon goblet.
791-792. No. 4516 and No. 4579 plates.
793. No. 4580 cup and saucer.
794. No. 4587 salt and pepper.
795. No. 4518 bon bon.
796. No. 4574 flower bowl, crimped.

797. Small covered jar from No. 4548 condiment set.
798. No. 5422 3-pc. mayonnaise set.
799. No. 4582 low sherbet.
800. No. 4457 2-light candle.
801. No. 4583 oil and vinegar with tray.
802. No. 4586 3-pc. individual sugar and cream with tray.
803. No. 4532 sugar and cream with tray.
804. No. 4524 2-handled bon bon.
805. No. 4575 ivy vase.
806. No. 4577 jam jar and cover.
807. No. 4541 6" candy box and cover.
808. Cheese comport from No. 4528 set.

All of these are products of H. Northwood Co.

809. Russet No. 713 footed bowl.
810. Blue Iris No. 696 candlesticks.
811. Blue Iris No. 647 bowl on black base.
812. Jade Green No. 694 bowl on black base.
813-814. Blue Iris and Russet No. 643 jelly or bon bon and cover.

815. Topaz Iris footed comport.
816. Topaz Iris footed salver.
817. Russet No. 645 footed bowl.
818. Topaz Iris covered sugar (called Barbella by collectors).
819-820. Topaz Iris and Blue Iris No. 675 handled candlesticks.

All of these Jade Green items were made by H. Northwood
Co. in 1924–25.
821. No. 643 jelly or bon bon and cover.
822. No. 657 candlesticks.
823. No. 647 bowl with white base.
824. No. 652 footed comport.
825. Twisted candlesticks.

826. No. 692 bowl (note twisted interior) on black base.
827. No. 727 twisted vase.
828. No. 675 handled candlestick.
829. No. 685 sherbet and No. 729 plate.
830. Cup from No. 722 plate/cup set.
831. No. 691 covered almond dish.
832. No. 698 handled sandwich tray.

Except for Fig. 835, these Chinese Coral items were made by H. Northwood Co. in 1924–25.

833. No. 708 candlesticks.
834. No. 678 bowl with black foot.
835. Fenton Mandarin Red No. 888 vase.
836. No. 643 jelly or bon bon and cover.

837-838. No. 707 bowls (note color differences).
839. No. 707 cupped bulb bowl.
840. Cup from No. 722 plate cup set.
841. No. 652 footed comport.
842. No. 641 fruit bowl.
843. No. 656 footed comport.
844. No. 698 handled sandwich tray.

Except as indicated, these are products of the Paden City
Glass Manufacturing Co.
845. Blue No. 701 footed comport.
846. Mulberry No. 114 candlestick.
847. Ebony No. 115 9" candlestick.
848. Green No. 503 fan vase.
849. Mulberry No. 117 candlestick.
850. Amber No. 115 7" candlestick.
851. Green No. 191 covered comport.

852. Cheriglo No. 700 tray with deep plate etching.
853. Amber No. 15 decanter, four wine glasses and tray (made
   by the New Martinsville Glass Manufacturing Co.).
854. Topaz vase (made from candy jar base) with cut
   decoration.
855. Cheriglo No. 207 sandwich tray.
856. Amber No. 701 covered candy jar with cut decoration.
857. Cheriglo No. 300 sandwich tray with deep plate etching.

858

859

860

861

862

863

864

863

865

866

867

868

All of these are products of the Paden City Glass Manufacturing Co.

858. Crystal No. 444 covered candy box.

859-861. Crystal No. 201 Spiral Optic sugar base, spooner and cream.

862. Crystal sponge cup.

863. Crystal No. 300 candlesticks with decal decoration.

864. Crystal No. 881 Gadroon bowl with decal decoration.

865. Crystal No. 612 square candlestick with cut decoration.

866. Crystal No. 612 square candlestick with cut decoration.

867. Crystal sandwich tray with octagonal handle.

868. Crystal cheese dish (goes with cracker tray).

869

870

871

872

873

874

875

All of these are products of the Paden City Glass
Manufacturing Co.
869. Crystal No. 215 tray.
870. Crystal No. 191 footed bowl with orange decoration.
871. Crystal No. 881 Gadroon tray.

872. Satin finished No. 220 crystal tray.
873. Crystal No. 1504 server with decoration.
874. Crystal No. 330 cheese and cracker set.
875. Crystal No. 700 sandwich tray (note decoration).

876   877   878   879   880

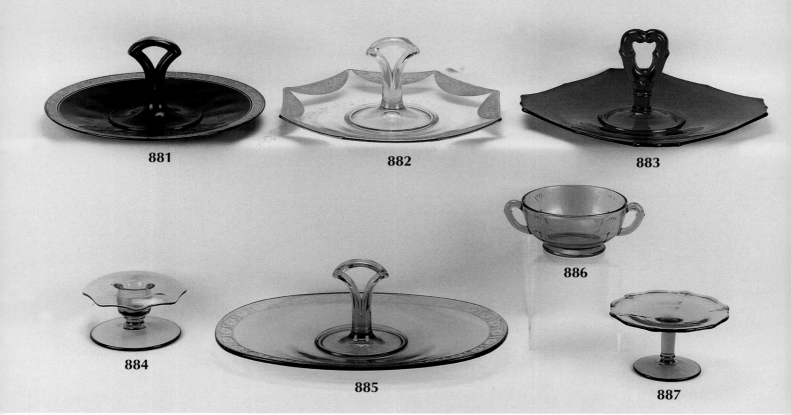

881   882   883

886

884   885   887

All of these are products of the Paden City Glass
Manufacturing Co.
876. Blue foot for No. 6 percolator.
877. Ebony No. 215 (cover only) with deep plate etching.
878. Ruby No. 69 Georgian tumbler.
879. Ruby No. 12 triangular ashtray.
880. Ebony No. 700 cigarette holder with metal cover.
881. Ebony sandwich tray with gold decoration.

882. Green No. 700 octagonal sandwich tray with gold
decoration.
883. Ruby No. 555 sandwich tray.
884. Amber No. 701 candlestick.
885. Amber No. 700 sandwich tray (note handle shape)
with gold decoration.
886. Amber No. 890 cream soup.
887. Amber No. 890 cheese comport.

All of these are products of the L. E. Smith Glass Co.

888-889. Black No. 800/4 7¹/₂" footed urn vases with very scarce cover (note low relief pattern near top of base).

890. Black No. 433/4-C crimped vase with dancing figures (note square foot)

891. Black No. 102/4 vase with silver bands.

892. Black No. 432 crimped vase.

893. Black hanging vase with chain.

894. Black No. 1012 bowl (mould purchased from Greensburg Glass Works).

895. Black powder box (called "Ripple" by collectors) with jade green figural cover (called "Jackie" by collectors).

896. Pink powder box base with black flower block.

897. Pink powder box base with pink flower block.

898. Black No. 1022 three-footed console bowl (note worn decoration).

899. Black footed urn vase with cover (note "veined onyx" decoration).

900. Black No. 1022 three-footed console bowl (note "veined onyx" decoration).

901

902

903

904

905

906

907

908

909

910

Except as indicated, these are products of the L. E. Smith Glass Co.

901. Green No. 100 small fan vase.

902. Amber No. 100 large fan vase.

903. Green No. 100 medium fan vase.

904. Black No. 675 cookie jar with worn decoration (mould purchased from Greensburg Glass Works).

905. Black base for No. 100 octagonal bowl.

906. Amber No. 100 12-inch octagonal bowl and base.

907. Green two-piece luncheon set (note moulded crackle effect).

908. Crystal No. 555 English Hobnail covered candy jar made by the Westmoreland Glass Co.

909. Opaque white No. 105 covered candy jar.

910. Crystal candlestick with bobeche and prisms (from No. 1/18 console set).

911   912   912   913   914

915   916   917   918   919

920   921   922

Unless otherwise indicated, these United States Glass Company products were called "Mother of Pearl," a color which debuted in 1912 and was made for a number of years.

911. No. 15310 high footed comport.

912. Crystal candlesticks with integral bobeche (probably made by U. S. Glass).

913. No. 151 candlestick (note shape of foot).

914. No. 151 candlestick (note shape of foot).

915. No. 189 covered candy jar.

916. No. 319 handled candlestick.(note decoration).

917. No. 56 colonial-style candlestick with oval foot (note decoration).

918. No. 179 flower bowl.

919. No. 179 sweet pea vase on black base.

920. No. 151 sweet pea vase.

921. No. 8076 11" open work orange bowl on black base.

922. No. 315 low foot comport.

Most of the items shown here are a United States Glass Company color originally called Red, but collectors typically refer to it as "amberina" today.

923. No. 310 6" basket.
924. No. 8076 open work orange bowl.
925. No. 315 7" high footed comport.
926. Crystal plate with Pomona decoration.
927. No. 315 low footed comport.

928. No. 310 11" open work fruit bowl.
929. Crystal No. 189 mayonnaise bowl (note optic) with plate (note decoration).
930. No. 179 sundae.
931. Bowl for No. 310 mayonnaise set.
932. No. 212 automobile vase.
933. No. 179 9" low footed comport.

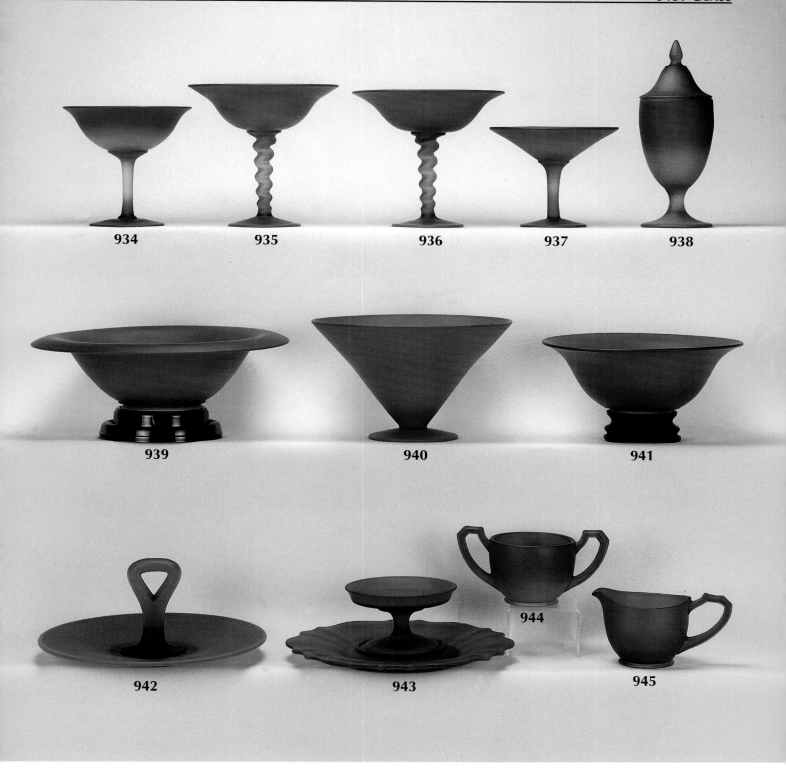

934.

935.

936.

937.

938.

939.

940.

941.

942.

943.

944.

945.

The items shown here are a United States Glass Company color originally called Red, but collectors typically refer to it as "amberina" today; all of these are satin finished.

934. No. 4721 flared grape fruit.

935. No. 315 7" high footed comport (note shape of foot).

936. No. 315 7" high footed comport (note variation in height).

937. No. 3201 6" comport.

938. No. 179 covered candy jar.

939. No. 8096 console bowl and base.

940. No. 179 9" regular comport.

941. Console bowl from No. 300 console set.

942. No. 179 handled cake plate.

943. No. 310 cheese and cracker set.

944-945. No. 179 sugar and cream.

946   947   948

949   950   951

952   953   954   955

Unless otherwise indicated, these are United States Glass Company products.

946. Amberina No. 179 7¹/₂" high footed comport.

947. Crystal covered pitcher and four handled tumblers (these have a craquelle effect, and applied blue handles/foot).

948. Amberina No. 151 sweet pea vase.

949. Amber candlesticks (probably made by U. S. Glass).

950. Mulberry No. 76 candlesticks.

951. Amber No. 87 candlesticks (note the original "pendants" on the integral bobeche; see Fig. 912).

952. Green No. 310 8¹/₂" open work comport.

953. Sapphire No. 79 6" candlestick.

954. Sapphire No. 8105 rolled edge salad bowl.

955. Amber No. 310 conic covered candy jar.

All of these are United States Glass Company products. At various points during the 1920s, the company called this color Topaz, Yellow or Canary; some items are satin finished.
956. No. 179 10" flared dahlia vase.
957. No. 3201 6" footed comport.
958. No. 179 7½" high footed comport.
959. No. 315 7" high footed comport.

960. No. 151 candlestick.
961. No. 179 9½" twisted candlesticks.
962. No. 189 low footed comport.
963. No. 179 9½" twisted candlesticks.
964. No. 310 flared berry bowl and black base.
965. No. 10 open work bowl.
966. Celery with black trim.

Several opaque colors—Coral Red, Jade Green and Pearl Blue—were introduced by the United States Glass Company in 1921. Notice the color variations of the Jade Green items shown on this page.

967. No. 179 sweet pea vase.
968. No. 179 sweet pea vase.
969. No. 151 6" dahlia vase.
970. Ivory No. 151 6" dahlia vase.

971. No. 151 small flared lily vase.
972. No. 151 10½" dahlia vase.
973. No. 179 9" centerpiece on black base.
974. No. 179 low foot comport.
975. No. 179 low foot comport.
976. No. 179 lily bowl on black base.
977. No. 179 lily bowl.
978. No. 151 plate.
979. No. 10 low candleholders.

980

981

982

983

984

985

986

987

988

989

990

The United States Glass Company introduced Coral Red in 1921.
980. No. 151 candlesticks.
981. Deep rolled edge bowl (original number not known).
982. No. 151 10½" flared dahlia vase.
983. No. 151 8" flared dahlia vase.
984. No. 179 9½" lily bowl on black base.

985. No. 179 sweet pea vase.
986. No. 310 centerpiece on black base,
987. No. 310 sweet pea vase on black base.
988. No. 10 open work flat bowl on black base.
989. No. 10 low candleholders.
990. No. 179 9½" lily bowl.

991 992 993 994 995 994

996 997 998 999

1000 1001 1002

All of these are products of the United States Glass Co. Original color names, when known, are provided.

991. Pearl Blue No. 151 8" cupped dahlia vase.
992. Pearl Blue No. 151 10½" cupped dahlia vase.
993. Pearl Blue No. 151 6" flared dahlia vase.
994. Pearl Blue No. 328 candlesticks.
995. Pearl Blue console bowl on Pearl Blue base.

996. Pearl Blue No. 8098 rose bowl on base.
997. No. 8098 rose bowl on base.
998. No. 179 sweet pea vase (possibly Pearl Blue, although one trade journal mentions Pearl Gray).
999. No. 179 centerpiece (very dark red, almost black).
1000. Ivory No. 179 sweet pea vase.
1001. No. 151 lily bowl.
1002. No. 151 lily bowl.

1003.   1004.   1005.   1006.

1007   1008   1007

1009   1009A   1009

All of these are products of the United States Glass Co.
1003. Black base.
1004. No. 9320 black base.
1005. Black base.
1006. Black base (note satin finish).
1007. Black satin finished No. 93 low candleholders with gold decoration and trim.

1008. Black No. 8105 rolled edge bowl on black base (note decoration).
1009. Royal Blue No. 79 6" candlesticks with gold trim.
1009A. Royal Blue No. 8096 console bowl with gold trim on black base.

1010   1011   1012   1013

1014   1015   1016

1017   1018   1019

All of these are products of the Viking Glass Co. Although Viking did not begin until 1944, it carried forward production using many New Martinsville moulds from earlier years.

1010. Crystal No. 4273 lazy susan set on metal base.
1011. Amber No. 5270 Princess covered treasure jar.
1012. Crystal No. 5226 Princess 11" cake salver.
1013. Crystal No. 5213 Princess candlestick.
1014. Crystal No. 5269 Princess 10" footed bowl.

1015. Crystal No. 5246 Princess 11" sandwich tray (see Fig. 1017; note different handle).
1016. Crystal No. 5224 Princess salver.
1017. Crystal No. 5246 Princess 11" sandwich tray with deep plate etching.
1018. Crystal No. 5213 candlestick with gold decoration.
1019. Crystal No. 5232 Princess cheese and cracker with deep plate etching.

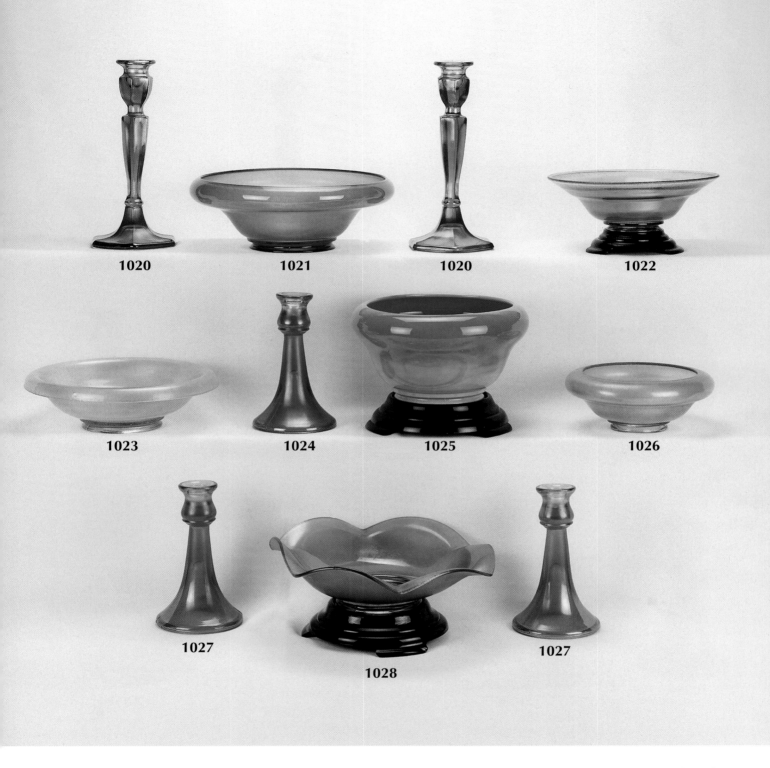

1020   1021   1020   1022

1023   1024   1025   1026

1027   1028   1027

All of these are products of the Vineland Flint Glass Co. The company's original name for iridescent blue was "Tut Blue," so that term is used here.

1020. Tut Blue candlesticks (made in three-part mould; the similar Fenton candlestick is made in a two-part mould).

1021. Tut Blue flared and cupped edge console bowl.

1022. Tut Blue flared console bowl on black base.

1023. Iridescent blue-green console bowl with rolled edge.

1024. Tut Blue candlestick.

1025. Opaque blue flared and cupped edge console bowl.

1026. Iridescent blue-green flared and cupped edge console bowl.

1027. Tut Blue candlesticks.

1028. Tut Blue crimped console bowl on black base.

1029

1030

1029

1031

1032

1033

1034

1033

1035

1036

1035

1037

All of these iridescent Wisteria items are products of the Vineland Flint Glass Co.

1029. Candlesticks.
1030. Console bowl with flared edge and black base.
1031. Bowl with flared edge.
1032. Console bowl with flared edge (note the original paper label on underside!).

1033. Candlesticks.
1034. Console bowl with flared and cupped edge and black base.
1035. Candlesticks.
1036. Console bowl with cupped edge and black base.
1037. Crimped console bowl on black base.

1038.   1039.   1040.   1041.   1042.   1043.

1044.   1045.   1046.

1047.   1048.   1049.   1050.

Except as indicated, these are products of the Westmoreland Glass Company.

1038. Crystal No. 1700 covered candy jar with all-over blue decoration and black trim.

1039. Topaz/Canary Yellow No. 1849 lemon tray.

1040. Crystal candlestick with blue decoration and gold trim.

1041. Amber No. 1211 butter ball with cut decoration.

1042. Crystal No. 1820 low foot comport with decoration.

1043. Crystal No. 1800 butter ball with orange and gold decoration.

1044. Crystal No. 1800 sandwich tray with decoration.

1045. Satin finished amber No. 1800 mayonnaise with decoration.

1046. Crystal No. 1800 sandwich tray with decoration (pre-1922).

1047. Crystal mayonnaise bowl and underplate with decoration (made by Duncan-Miller).

1048. Blue Shell nappy, no toes (possibly Westmoreland, but probably New Martinsville).

1049. Green No. 1708 covered candy box.

1050. Crystal covered bowl with decoration.

All of these are products of the Westmoreland Glass Co.

1051. Crystal No. 1707 covered candy jar with cutting and amber stain decoration.

1052. Crystal No. 1707 candy jar base with cutting and amber stain decoration.

1053. Crystal No. 1707 covered candy jar with cutting and amber stain decoration.

1054. Crystal high foot sweetmeat with cutting and amber stain decoration.

1055. Black No. 1865 bowl with gold decoration.

1056. Opaque blue bowl on black base.

1057. Amber No. 1707 covered candy jar.

1058. Blue No. 1031 flower bowl stand.

1059. Green No. 1031 flower bowl stand.

1060. Blue No. 1031/0 flower bowl stand.

1061. Dark amber No. 1503 covered sugar or bon bon.

1062. Roselin No. 1211 Octagon sandwich tray with cutting and gold decoration.

1063

1064

1065

1066

1067

1068

1069

1070

1071

1072

1073

1074

All of these are products of the Westmoreland Glass Company.

1063. Ruby lustre night set (also called tumble-up).

1064. Crystal No. 1826 mayonnaise, No. 1801 serving platter and No. 1800 ladle (all have all-over orange decoration which has been cut through as well as black trim).

1065. Crystal No. 1826 mayonnaise with all-over yellow decoration and gold decoration.

1066. Crystal No. 1910 tall comport with all-over yellow decoration, black foot and black trim.

1067. Crystal No. 1865 bowl with orange decoration and Charles West's patented lattice decoration on black No. 1031/0 flower bowl stand.

1068. Opaque white No. 1826 mayonnaise with decoration.

1069. Crystal no. 1800 cheese comport with orange decoration and gold trim.

1070. Crystal No. 1800 sandwich tray with yellow decoration and gold trim.

1071. Crystal No. 1849 butter ball with yellow decoration and gold trim.

1072. Crystal No. 1849 butter ball with yellow decoration and gold trim.

1073-1074. Crystal No. 1503 covered sugar or bon bon and No. 1707 covered candy jar (note all-over orange decoration as well as handpainted decoration and gold trim).

RUBY WITH CRYSTAL HANDLES REFRESHMENT SETS
(Dec. B & L 10, Platinum Bands)

1076

No. 457/457—10 oz.

1075

1078

1077

No. 451/840—10 oz.

1080

No. 456/455—6 oz.

1079

1082

No. 455/455—10 oz.

1081

1084

No. 453/453—9 oz.

1083

1085

No. 400/400—6 oz. Ruby Punch Bowl Set
With 11 in. Plate
Dec. B & L 1-C
With Coin Gold Bands

1086

No. 400/400—6 oz. Ritz Blue Punch Bowl Set
With 11 in. Plate
Dec. B & L 1 Platinum Bands

WINE DECANTER SETS

1087
1088
1089
1090

No. 8 Crystal
Using either No. 300—3 oz. Stem Wine or
No. 540—3 oz. Sham Tumbler
Dec. B & L 104
Lavender Ice with Platinum Bands

No. 4 Decanter
Ruby with Crystal Stopper
Dec. B & L 114
Platinum Dots and Bands

1091
1092
1093

No. 7 Crystal
Using either No. 415—3 oz. Stem Wine or
No. 741—3 oz. Sham Tumbler
Dec. B & L 17
Crystal Ice with Platinum Bands

1094
1095

No. 2 Crystal
With No. 5041—4 oz. Stem Wine
Dec. B & L 11
Crystal Ice with Platinum Bands

1096
1097

No. 2 Ruby
With Crystal Stopper using
No. 1000—3 oz. Wine Crystal Bowl
and Stem with Ruby Foot
Dec. B & L 15
Platinum Bands

1098
1099

No. 7 Crystal
With No. 415—3 oz. Stem Wine
Dec. B & L 12
Crystal Ice with Platinum Bands

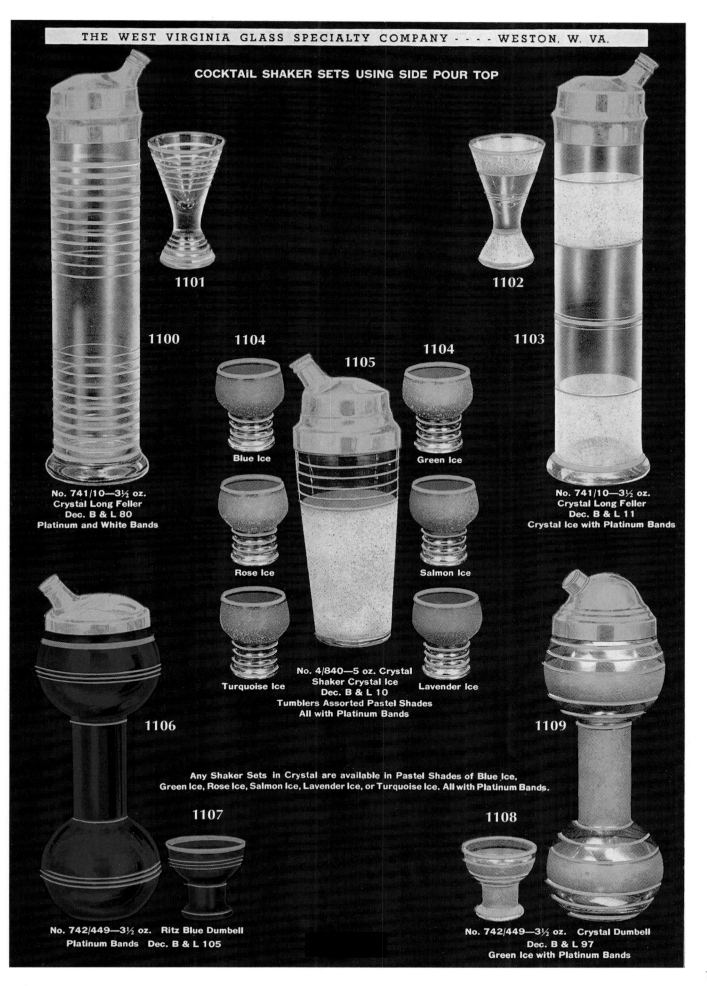

COCKTAIL SHAKER SETS USING SIDE POUR TOP

1101

1102

1100

1104

1105

1104

1103

Blue Ice

Green Ice

No. 741/10—3½ oz.
Crystal Long Feller
Dec. B & L 80
Platinum and White Bands

Rose Ice

Salmon Ice

No. 741/10—3½ oz.
Crystal Long Feller
Dec. B & L 11
Crystal Ice with Platinum Bands

Turquoise Ice

No. 4/840—5 oz. Crystal
Shaker Crystal Ice
Dec. B & L 10
Tumblers Assorted Pastel Shades
All with Platinum Bands

Lavender Ice

1106

1109

Any Shaker Sets in Crystal are available in Pastel Shades of Blue Ice,
Green Ice, Rose Ice, Salmon Ice, Lavender Ice, or Turquoise Ice. All with Platinum Bands.

1107

1108

No. 742/449—3½ oz.   Ritz Blue Dumbell
Platinum Bands   Dec. B & L 105

No. 742/449—3½ oz.   Crystal Dumbell
Dec. B & L 97
Green Ice with Platinum Bands

143

THE WEST VIRGINIA GLASS SPECIALTY COMPANY - - - - WESTON, W. VA.

1110

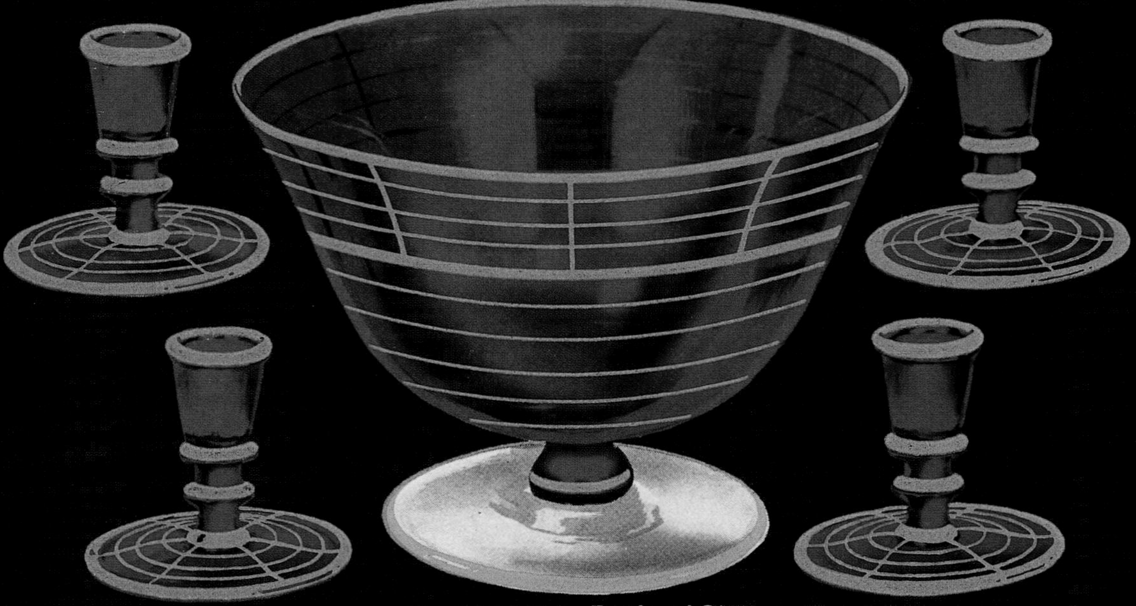

No. 1100 Ruby Bowl and Stem
With Crystal Foot Console Bowl
Using Four Ruby Candleholders
Dec. B & L 17-H
Platinum Bands

1111

No. 105 Vase
Ruby Bowl with Crystal Foot
Dec. B & L 57
Platinum Bands

1112

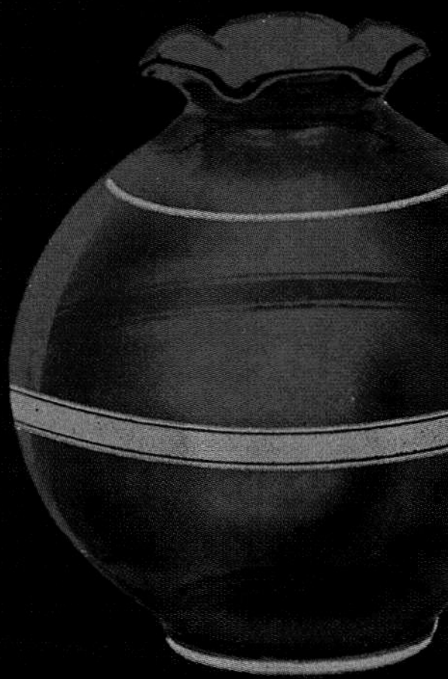

No. 48—6 in. Crimpt Top Ruby Vase
Dec. B & L 2
Platinum Bands

1113

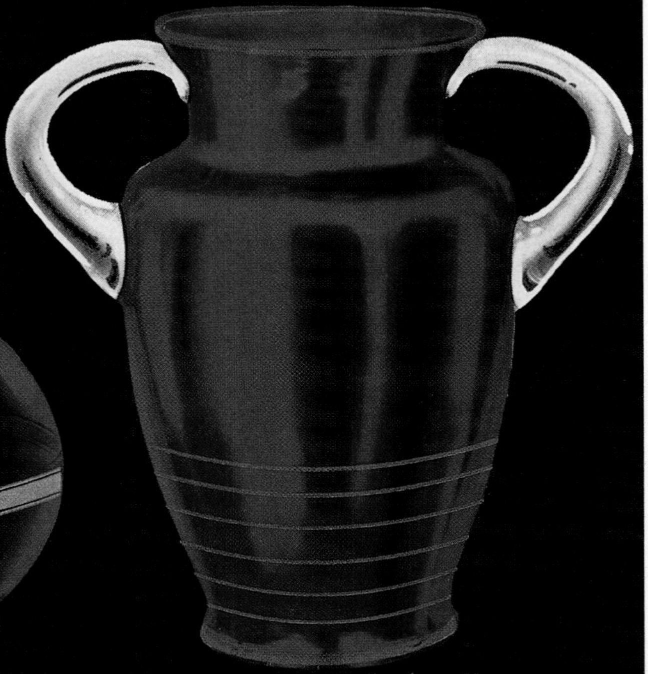

No. 20—10 in. Vase
Ruby Bowl with Two Crystal Handles
Dec. B & L 29
Bright Gold Bands

FOSTORIA GLASS COMPANY
MOUNDSVILLE, WEST VIRGINIA

Fostoria Glass Company
MANUFACTURERS OF

Fostoria
MADE IN U.S.A.

FINE TABLE GLASSWARE
Moundsville, W. Va., U.S.A.

C. B. ROE, PRESIDENT
W. F. DALZELL, VICE PRESIDENT
A. W. KOENEMUND, SECRETARY

January 30, 1933.

This glassmaking firm takes its name from the town where it was born, namely, Fostoria, Ohio. The company began in the 1880s, and like the other glass tableware plants in the Findlay-Fostoria "gas boom" area of northwestern Ohio, the Fostoria Glass company turned out pattern glass sets and novelties. By the early 1890s, gas supplies were dwindling rapidly, so the operation was relocated in 1892 to a new plant built in Moundsville, West Virginia. About a decade later, when the National Glass Company closed one of its plants in Findlay, William Dalzell (who preferred to use the initials "W. A. B." before his surname) left the National's employ to become

president of the Fostoria Glass Company in its new location; he was the first of several Dalzell men to lead Fostoria's fortunes.

For the first decade and a half of the twentieth century, Fostoria produced pattern glass sets in pressed ware as well as blown stemware which was decorated with needle etching or deep plate etching. Some cutting was also done. In early 1915, Fostoria introduced its No. 2056 line. Dubbed "American" (perhaps to capture the feelings of patriotism stirred by WWI), this large line became Fostoria's mainstay for decades to come. In the 1920s, two other pattern lines, No. 2350 Pioneer and No. 2375 Fairfax, also took on important roles, and colonial-style pressed ware pieces were made to compete with similar items made by many other firms.

By the standards of other companies, Fostoria's production of color is relatively modest. Amber, blue, canary and green were being made by the mid-1920s. Later in the decade, Fostoria's colors took on more fanciful names—Azure, Ebony, Orchid, Rose (Dawn) and Topaz. Some iridescent ware, called "Mother of Pearl," was also made in the 1920s. In the 1930s, ruby was

Fostoria Glass Works, Moundsville, W. Va.

American Pattern No. 2056

A unique design made into a decidedly attractive and complete line of tableware of comparatively light weight.

It is the most original and brilliant pressed pattern on the market today.

It is carefully made and carefully selected.

Illustrations and prices furnished promptly on request.

In Lead Blown

We have new shapes in Stemware, new patterns in Cutting, new patterns in Needle and Deep Plate Etchings, Iridescent and new Coin Gold decorations.

Samples on display in our salesrooms

FOSTORIA GLASS COMPANY
MOUNDSVILLE, WEST VIRGINIA

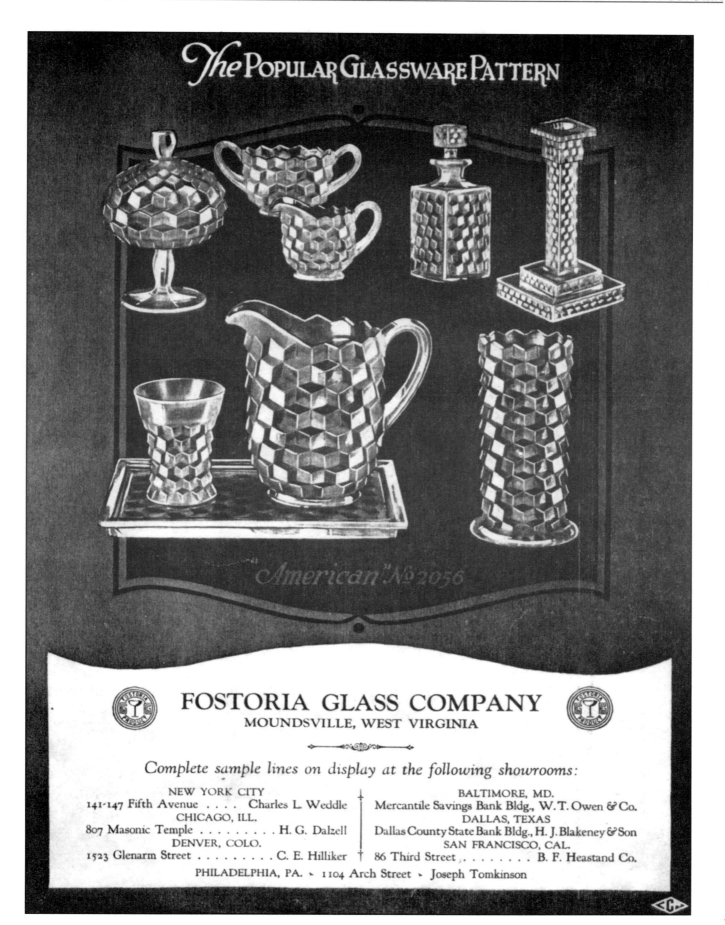

added to the color chart, and Burgundy and Wisteria also appeared.

Decorations, particularly needle etchings, continued to be featured by Fostoria in the 1920s, but these were relatively expensive to produce, and machine made tableware was starting to rival the quality of these designs. New deep plate etchings were introduced regularly, but each of these seemed to last only a few years in the marketplace before another took its place and competed for attention with the similar products of many other factories. In the 1930s, cut decorations assumed greater importance in the Fostoria line.

The No. 2419 Mayfair line was introduced in the early 1930s, followed by No. 2440 Lafayette, No. 2449 Hermitage, No. 2496 Baroque, No. 2510 Sunray, No. 2560 Coronet and No. 2574 Raleigh. These were generally "dinnerware" lines, but some, such as Baroque, included elaborate candelabras and other decorative pieces.

The Fostoria Glass Company survived the Depression Era as well as the difficult 1950s (which claimed the Cambridge and Heisey firms), but the 1980s brought Fostoria's closure. Kenneth Dalzell, who was associated with the firm, started Dalzell-Viking Corp. and began making glass in the old Viking/New Martinsville plant.

Fostoria's earliest history is well-recorded in Melvin L. Murray's *Fostoria, Ohio, Glass II* (available from Antique Publications). Hazel Marie Weatherman's *Fostoria: Its First Fifty Years* (published in 1972) provides a good overview of the 1920s and 1930s.

FOSTORIA GLASS COMPANY
Moundsville, W. Va., U. S. A.

"THREE BEAUTIES"

STADLER PHOTO CO. CHICAGO.

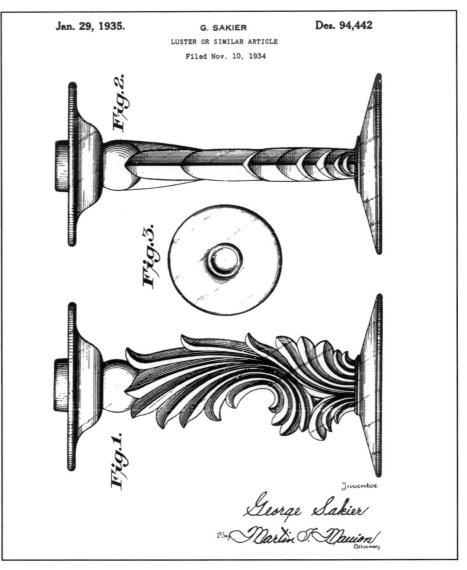

Jan. 29, 1935.　　G. SAKIER　　Des. 94,442

LUSTER OR SIMILAR ARTICLE

Filed Nov. 10, 1934

Fig. 2.

Fig. 3.

Fig. 1.

Inventor

George Sakier

By Martin J. Manion
Attorney

H. C. FRY GLASS COMPANY
ROCHESTER, PENNSYLVANIA

Although perhaps best known for its cut glass and heat-resistant oven glass, the H. C. Fry Glass Co. also manufactured some noteworthy colored glass during the 1920s. The firm's namesake was Henry Clay Fry, a Kentucky native who was employed by several glass companies in the Pittsburgh area before serving in the Union army during the Civil War.

From the early 1870s until 1900, Fry was president of the Rochester Tumbler Co. in Rochester, Pa. This was among the largest glass plants in the nation, and it may have been the first to use natural gas as fuel. Fry was instrumental in the formation of the National Glass Co. in 1898-99, but he left this organization after the National changed its plans to rebuild the Rochester Tumbler concern after a disastrous fire.

In 1901 Fry and his two sons founded the Rochester Glass Company, but the name was soon changed to the H. C. Fry Glass Co. The company went into receivership in the mid-1920s, and, after Fry died in 1929, the company was reorganized. It went out of business in 1933, but its plant was leased to the Libbey Glass Co. of Toledo for a brief period.

In the 1920s, the Fry enterprise made colored glass pitchers and tumblers which are quite similar to those made by Fenton and other manufacturers. Fry also made a distinctive sandwich tray and console sets with handpainted decorations. Colors mentioned in Fry's Catalogue No. 10 and other sources include the following: amber, Azure blue, black, canary, Emerald, Fuschia, Golden Glow, green, Rose and Royal blue. Crackled ware was made in crystal and Golden Glow

For more information on Fry glass, consult the H. C. Fry Glass Society's excellent book, *The Collector's Encyclopedia of Fry Glassware* (Paducah: Collector Books, 1990).

**Postcard
view of the
H. C. Fry plant.**

Manufactured by
H. C. FRY GLASS CO.
ROCHESTER, PA.

5941

1290

1291

5942

1288

5943

1289

1292

5944

TABLEWARE
Fine Quality Hand Blown Tableware in
Graceful Shapes and Designs

No.	Coupons	No.	Coupons
1288—Water Tumblers. Height 3¾ inches. Set of six	625	**1290—Footed Sherbets.** Height 4¼ inches. Set of six	825
1289—Iced Tea Glasses. Height 5¼ inches. Set of six	750	**1291—Goblets.** Height 6½ inches. Set of six	825
5941—Wine Glasses. Height 4¾ inches. Set of six	775	**1292—Pitcher.** Capacity 2 quarts	825
5942—Beverage Glasses. Height 4 inches. Set of six	775	**5943—Footed Water Tumblers.** Height 4½ inches. Set of six	825
		5944—Footed Iced Tea Glasses. Height 5¼ inches. Set of six	925

DO NOT SEAL PACKAGE SENT BY THIRD OR FOURTH CLASS MAIL.

Fry glass was often used as premium items. This pieces, which retain their original factory items numbers,
appeared in a United Profit Sharing Corporation premium book for 1930-31.

HAZEL-ATLAS GLASS COMPANY
WHEELING, WEST VIRGINIA

The city address of this firm is a bit misleading. Although the corporate headquarters and sales offices of the Hazel-Atlas Glass company were located in Wheeling, the enterprise actually embraced several glass factories in various states (Oklahoma, Pennsylvania and West Virginia), but all were under the watchful eyes of the Brady brothers--Charles, Joseph and William. The old Hazel-Atlas building still stands in downtown Wheeling today, serving West Virginia Northern Community College.

Early on, the key plants, separately named Hazel and Atlas, were located in Washington, Pennsylvania, and the key products were wide-mouth containers and fruit jars made by automatic machines. The company name Hazel-Atlas was adopted in 1902, and the plant at Clarksburg, West Virginia, emerged as the focal point for household glassware over the next two decades.

The company did not begin to produce tableware until the early 1930s, but the transition was relatively easy, and the automatic machines produced a daunting quantity of goods. Among the Depression era patterns attributed to Hazel-Atlas are these: Aurora, Cloverleaf, Colonial Block, Florentine (two versions), Fruits, Moderntone, New Century, Newport, Ovide, Ribbon, Roxana, Royal Lace, Ships/Sailboat, Starlight and X-Design. Production of most tableware lines slacked off during WWII and some were discontinued, but the postwar years brought expansion to Hazel-Atlas.

In the mid-1950s, Hazel-Atlas was purchased by the Continental Can Company , and it became the Hazelware division of that firm. Eventually the Clarksburg tableware plant changed hands several times before its closure in the 1980s.

There is excellent coverage of the Hazel-Atlas story by Marg Iwen in two articles for *Glass Collector's Digest* (October/November, 1996 and December/January, 1997).

The Success Butter or Sugar

Best Value on the Market Today

Can be retailed for Ten Cents with a profit
Wide awake buyers get busy. Open the new year right with a special

WM. LANDBERG & CO.
GLASSWARE SPECIALTIES
Manufacturers of Light Cut Blown and Pressed Glasswares
112 Bowery, New York City
Our Mr. Sam. Landberg will be at the Fort Pitt in January

(above) Hazel-Atlas butterdish appears in a glass jobber's ad; (at right) postcard view of a Labor Day parade in Washington, Pa., as Hazel-Atlas workers march by.

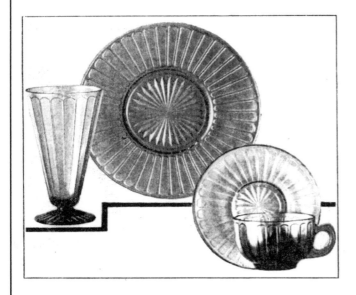

A. H. HEISEY AND COMPANY
NEWARK, OHIO

This firm's namesake was Augustus H. Heisey, who had been associated with the George Duncan & Sons organization in Pittsburgh from the 1870s until about 1894. Heisey built a plant at Newark, Ohio, and glassmaking commenced in 1896. Heisey's three sons—George Duncan Heisey, Edgar W. Heisey and Thomas C. Heisey—were involved in the business.

During the last few years of the nineteenth century and the first decade of the twentieth, the Heisey firm produced a number of pattern glass tableware sets as well as other utilitarian items. These were typically in crystal glass, but Heisey did make a separate line of opaque glass called Ivorina Verde. During the 1920s, Heisey made a great variety of products, ranging from elegant stemware and high-quality tableware to soda fountain ware and ash trays.

During the 1920s and 1930s, Heisey introduced a number of new patterns. Some were short-lived, while others remained in production for many years, although the number of items varied from time to time. Still others were in production for a short time or a few years, and, after being discontinued for a time, were later reinstated in the Heisey line, sometimes enjoying greater popularity than that occasioned by their first appearance!

Here are the primary lines: No. 355 , No. 406-407, Tudor (No. 411-414), No. 473, No. 500, No. 1170, No. 1184-1189, No. 1229, No. 1231, No. 1252, Empress (No. 1401), Old Sandwich (No. 1404), Ipswich (No. 1405), Twentieth Century (No. 1415), Victorian (No. 1425), Warwick (No. 1428), Rococo (No. 1447), Quaker (No. 1463), Ridgeleigh (No. 1469), Stanhope (No. 1483), Saturn (No. 1485), Coleport (No. 1486), Kohinoor (No. 1488), and Fern (No. 1495).

Heisey introduced an interesting variety of transparent colors during the 1920s and 1930s, although production of colored ware did not begin in earnest until the late 1920s. The initial production color in 1925 was a green hue called Moongleam, and it was followed by Amber and a pink color called Flamingo. Many of the other Heisey color names are interesting ones: Alexandrite (lavender), Hawthorne (amethyst), Marigold (dark yellow), Sahara (light yellow), Stiegel Blue (cobalt), and Tangerine (orange-red). A very light yellow-green from the early 1920s is called "vaseline" by collectors today.

The Heisey plant closed in 1958, and moulds and other assets were purchased by the Imperial Glass Corporation of Bellaire, Ohio. Today, there is an enormous amount of information available on Heisey glass through the Heisey Museum in Newark, Ohio. A good book to consult is Neila Bredehoft's *Collector's Encyclopedia of Heisey Glass, 1925-1938*.

A. H. Heisey Glass Factory, Newark, Ohio.

Postcard view of the Heisey plant.

No. 1–300–1 LIGHT CANDELABRUM
Height 12″, with "A" Prisms

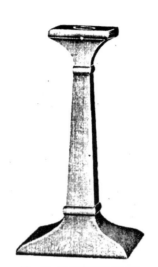

No. 21 CANDLESTICK
7″, 9″ and 11″ Sizes

No. 5 CANDLESTICK
5″, 6″, 7″, 8″, 9″
and 11″ Sizes

We make a complete line of the highest grade Glassware for the table. Also Candelabra, Candlesticks, Flower Vases, Decanters, Ice Cream Trays, etc.

We Guarantee That All Glassware Bearing Our *Trade-Mark Has No Equal*

CATALOGUE SENT ON APPLICATION

A. H. HEISEY & CO. (Incorporated) NEWARK, OHIO

TRADE H MARK

NEW YORK OFFICE:
25 West Broadway
PHILADELPHIA OFFICE:
610 Denckla Bldg., 11th and Market Sts.

BALTIMORE OFFICE:
122 West Baltimore St.
BOSTON OFFICE:
144 Congress St.

CHICAGO OFFICE: 510 Heyworth Bldg., 42 Madison St.

DESIGN.

A. J. SANFORD.
GLASS ARTICLE.
APPLICATION FILED JULY 8, 1919.

57,275.
Patented Mar. 8, 1921.

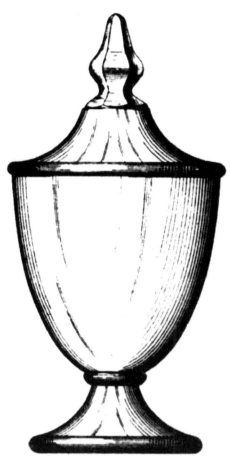

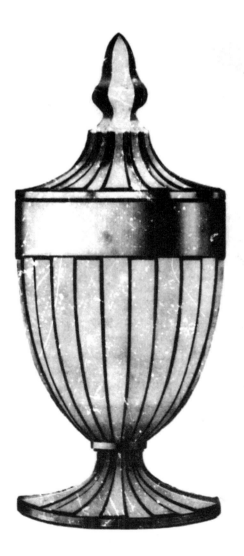

These Heisey candy jars
date from the early 1920s,
and the plain version was protected
by a design patent.

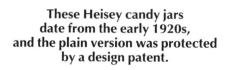

Dec. 8, 1925. Des. 68,966

T. C. HEISEY

CANDLESTICK

Filed March 17, 1923

Fig.1.

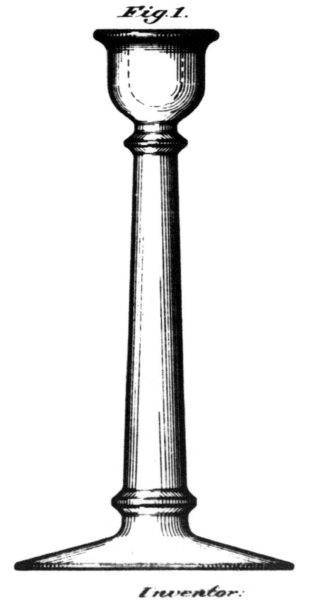

Inventor:
T CLARENCE HEISEY

Fenelon B Brock
Att'y.

Dec. 6, 1927. T. C. HEISEY Des. 74,012

CANDLESTICK

Filed Jan. 7. 1927

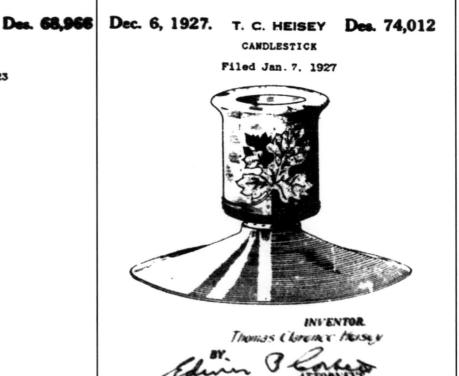

INVENTOR.
Thomas Clarence Heisey
BY
Edwin P Coler
ATTORNEYS.

Aug. 24 , 1926. T. C. HEISEY Des. 70,879

CANDLESTICK

Filed April 23. 1926

Thomas Clarence Heisey
INVENTOR.

Edwin P. Coler
ATTORNEYS.

158

HOCKING GLASS COMPANY
LANCASTER, OHIO

This important glass manufacturing company began in 1905 when Lucian B. Martin and his son, L. Philip Martin, combined with Isaac J. Collins to form a new corporation. All three men had been associated with the Ohio Flint Glass concern, which they had leased from the nearly bankrupt National Glass Company combine.

Lucien B. Martin, whose father Ebenezer had organized the town of Martins Ferry, was a glassman of long experience. He was a salesman for Hobbs-Brockunier in the 1870s, and he helped found the Fostoria Glass Company (then in Fostoria, Ohio) in the 1880s. In the mid-1890s, L. Philip Martin was a salesman for Fostoria (now in Moundsville, West Virginia), but both men became associated with the National Glass Company at the turn of the century, ultimately leasing the Ohio Flint Glass Works from the National. Collins had been manager of the decorating department at the Ohio Flint. Collins soon gained

control of the Hocking plant, and the Martin men left to form the Lancaster Glass Company.

At first the Hocking enterprise made decorated opal [milk glass] products; a year after the plant's inception, these were described as "novelties not generally attempted in anything but china and earthenware (*Glass and Pottery World*, January, 1907).

By the mid-1920s, Isaac "Ike" Collins and other investors had acquired several other plants in addition to the Hocking firm. The May 13, 1926, issue of *Pottery, Glass and Brass Salesman* mentioned the recent purchase of the Monongah Glass Co. plant by "the Collins group" and listed its other holdings: Hocking Glass Company, Lancaster Glass Company and the National Lens and Glass Company (all of Lancaster, Ohio); the Standard Glass Company of Bremen, Ohio; and the Steubenville, Ohio, plant of the Gill Bros. Company. A new organization, the Hocking Glass Sales Corporation, was formed to market the products

(*Text continued on page 163*) **159**

"Miss America" line

2508—14 oz.
Iced Tea

2506—10 oz.
Table Tumbler

2503—5 oz.
Fruit Juice

2514—3 oz.
Wine

2515—5½ oz.
Fruit Juice

2516—10 oz.
Footed Tumbler

2513 Footed Sherbet
2522—5¾ in. Plate

2562 Sugar

2561 Cream

2550 Cup
2551 Saucer

2560 Salt & Pepper
Chrome Top

2546 — 4¾ x 5½ in.
Footed Comport

2524 — 8½ in.
Salad Plate

2508—14 oz. Iced Tea
2552—5¾ in. Coaster

2526—10¼ in.
Dinner Plate

2535—5½ in.
Fruit or Cereal

2528—10¼ in.
Grill Plate

"Miss America" line

2545—8¾ in.
Relish

2567—12 in.
Cake Plate

2544—10½ in.
Celery Tray

2573—67 oz.
Jug

2539—8½ in.
Fruit Bowl

2566—12¼ in.
Meat Dish

2532—8½ in.
Rose Bowl

2547—10¼ in.
Vegetable Dish

2569—11½ in.
Candy Jar and Cover

THE POTTERY, GLASS & BRASS SALESMAN

"NORMANDIE" CRYSTAL

A New Brilliant Drinking Line

of the various factories, and it opened a newly furnished showroom in New York City at 129-313 Fifth Avenue.

The relationships among the factories are not easy to sort out. One ad (*Pottery, Glass and Brass Salesman*, August 11, 1927) reveals that Lancaster blanks were cut in the Breman plant. A later ad (*Pottery, Glass and Brass Salesman*, September 17, 1931) suggests that the Hocking plant made glass by automatic machine, while the Lancaster concern was semi-automatic and had an etching shop.

Hocking's Miss America was being advertised in March, 1933. Normandie was on the market during the fall of 1935, and Rose Lace Edge, advertised as "the most beautiful popular priced line ever put on the market," was available in March, 1936. Queen Mary came out in the fall of 1936.

In late 1937, the Hocking Glass Company was absorbed by the Anchor Cap Corporation, and the Anchor-Hocking Glass Corporation was formed.

ROSE LACE EDGE LINE

THE MOST BEAUTIFUL POPULAR PRICED LINE EVER PUT ON THE MARKET!

IMPERIAL GLASS CORPORATION
BELLAIRE, OHIO

Imperial Glass Corporation
MANUFACTURERS OF
QUALITY GLASSWARE

BELLAIRE, OHIO   Oct. 8, 1931.

This firm began in the fall of 1901 when ground was broken for the construction of a large tableware plant. The effort was the brainchild of Edward Muhleman, a Wheeling based financier who had recently sold his Crystal Glass Company to the National Glass Company combine. Progress was slow, and the concern did not begin to make glass until February or March, 1904.

Within a few years, Imperial was a major force in the glass tableware market. Beginning in 1908, the enterprise made huge quantities of iridescent ware and vied with Fenton, Dugan, and Northwood in this highly competitive area. Imperial made pressed and blown glassware of all sorts, including an imitation cut glass called NUCUT, and did virtually every kind of decorating: cutting, etching and sandblasting. Catalogs running to several hundred pages were not uncommon.

During the 1920s, Imperial was at the forefront of major trends with its introductions of new transparent (Golden Green and Rose Marie) and opaque colors as well as production of luncheon sets in new patterns and console sets (see Figs. 527-538). Stunning "Free Hand"

art glass was made by a group of European workers, and a line called Lead Lustre was developed. The plant's momentum was slowed with the death of a key executive (Victor Wicke), but, after a period of difficulties including receivership, it was reorganized as the Imperial Glass Corporation.

In the 1930s, two table service patterns in crystal—No. 400 Candlewick and No. 160 Cape Cod (see Figs. 509-526)—buoyed the company financially, and it continued to develop new colors and products.

Imperial bought moulds and fixtures from the Central Glass Company of Wheeling in 1939, and, about two decades later, Imperial acquired the assets of both A. H. Heisey and Company and the Cambridge Glass Company. For more information on Imperial's eighty-year history and production, see the *Imperial Glass Encyclopedia* (*Vol. I "A-Cane"* and *Vol. II "Cape Cod-L"*), published by Antique Publications in 1995 and 1997, respectively.

Candlewick creamer and sugar with original labels (the label is upside down on the sugar bowl). Probably used beginning in 1936, these silver and blue labels depict a Candlewick candleholder.

Sets illustrated consist of one 80 ounce pitcher and 12½ ounce tumblers, both HAND BLOWN

One-half dozen sets in bulk carton, Seven or nine piece Shipping weight 40 pounds

One set in individual carton, Seven or nine piece Shipping weight 10 pounds

451/cut 451.   7 piece Ice Tea Set,   Per set, $4.50
451/cut 451.   9 piece Ice Tea Set,   Per set, $5.60

Georgian tumbler and pitcher with cut decoration.

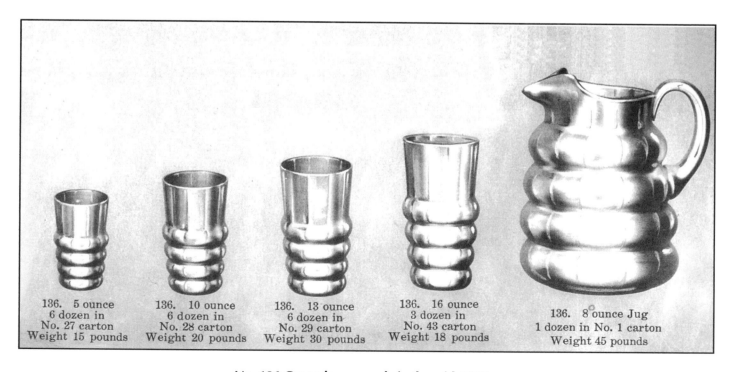

136.   5 ounce
6 dozen in
No. 27 carton
Weight 15 pounds

136.   10 ounce
6 dozen in
No. 28 carton
Weight 20 pounds

136.   13 ounce
6 dozen in
No. 29 carton
Weight 30 pounds

136.   16 ounce
3 dozen in
No. 43 carton
Weight 18 pounds

136.   8 ounce Jug
1 dozen in No. 1 carton
Weight 45 pounds

No. 136 Granada was made in the mid-1930s.

INDIANA GLASS COMPANY
DUNKIRK, INDIANA

ALL CONTRACTS SUBJECT TO CONTINGENCIES BEYOND OUR CONTROL. PRICES SUBJECT TO CHANGE WITHOUT NOTICE.
TRANSPORTATION RECEIPTS BEING EVIDENCE OF DELIVERY IN GOOD ORDER OUR RESPONSIBILITY CEASES.
WE PAY NO BILLS CONTRACTED BY AGENTS. MAKE ALL REMITTANCES DIRECT TO HOUSE.
IF NOT REMITTED WHEN DUE SUBJECT TO SIGHT DRAFT WITH EXCHANGE. NO CONTRACTS WITH AGENT BINDING UNTIL APPROVED BY US

FRANK W. MERRY
PRESIDENT

CHAS. L. GAUNT
VICE PRES.-SECY.

HENRY J. BATSCH
VICE PRESIDENT

INDIANA GLASS COMPANY
MANUFACTURERS OF
PRESSED AND BLOWN GLASSWARE

DUNKIRK, IND., U.S.A.

October 29, 1930.

EARL W. MERRY
TREASURER

GEO. W. HASKELL
SALES MANAGER

The history of glassmaking in Dunkirk, Indiana, goes back a long way, indeed, and the full story has yet to be told. The Beatty-Brady Glass Company moved from Steubenville, Ohio, to Dunkirk in the mid-1890s. The firm joined the National Glass Company combine in 1899, as did several other Indiana-based glass manufacturers.

When the National suffered financial reverses, the plant was leased to new management. It operated as the Indiana Glass Company beginning in 1904, and it was completely independent of the National and incorporated as a separate entity before 1910. In the 1920s and 1930s, the Indiana Glass Company produced a great variety of glass, ranging from tableware to such industrial items as automobile light lenses.

Indiana's No. 600 line, popularly called "Tea Room" by collectors today, was featured in a full page ad in *Pottery, Glass*

and Brass Salesman (December 15, 1927). The date suggests that No. 600 was probably Indiana's new line, scheduled for its debut at the January, 1928, glass show, as the glass factories typically showcased their new wares with ads at this time. Moreover, this important advertisement reveals the original name for Indiana's No. 600, namely, Centennial. What "centennial" was being celebrated in 1928? (incidentally, Florence incorrectly dates Tea Room from 1926).

Another well-known Indiana line is No. 610, which is generally called Pyramid by collectors. Florence dates this from 1926, but the U. S. Design Patent application forms were filed on January 6, 1931, by Jeddia B. Clark, who assigned the rights to his motif to the Indiana Glass company. The patents (#83, 846 and #83,895) were granted in

(Text continued on page 171)

No. 125 Berry Sugar

No. 125 Berry Cream

INDIANA GLASS CO.
Dunkirk, Indiana.

165 Berry Sugar

165 Berry Cream

MANUFACTURERS OF

Tableware, Lamps, Vases, Goblets, Soda Fountain Supplies

and

Decorated Ware, Both Fired and Cold Colors

EXPORT REPRESENTATIVE
GEO. B. HALL, 95 Chambers Street, New York City

SAMPLE ROOMS

NEW YORK, 200 5th Avenue Bldg.
BOSTON, 44 Federal Street
PHILADELPHIA, 1007 Filbert St.
DETROIT, 606 Congress Bldg.

BALTIMORE, 21 N. Liberty
ST. LOUIS, 325 Locust
CHICAGO, 17 N. Wabash
ST. PAUL, 538 Bremer Arcade

INDIANA GLASS CO.
DUNKIRK, INDIANA

Manufacturers of

Pressed and Blown Glassware
Crystal, Colored and Decorated

No. 172 Covered Candy Jar

Made in Crystal, Amber or Green

SAMPLE ROOMS:

New York: 200 Fifth Avenue   Chicago: 17 North Wabash Avenue
Philadelphia: 1007 Filbert Street   Boston: 93 Summer Street
Baltimore: 17 North Liberty Street   St. Louis: 516 Granite Building
Detroit: 524 Griswold Street   St. Paul: 538 Bremer Arcade

COMPLETE LINE WILL BE SHOWN DURING JANUARY AT FORT PITT HOTEL, PITTSBURGH, ROOMS 708-710

April, 1931 (Florence also dates No. 610 incorrectly, suggesting that it was introduced in 1926).

Also associated with Indiana are these lines: No. 170 Sandwich, No. 601 (Avocado), No. 612 (Horseshoe), No. 615 (Lorain or Basket), No. 616 (Vernon), and No. 618 (Pineapple and Floral) as well as Indiana Custard (patented 1933), Moderne Classic (c. 1934) and Old English.

The Indiana Glass factory is still in operation today, operating as an automatic machine plant under the ownership of the Lancaster Colony Corporation.

INDIANA GLASS WORKS, DUNKIRK, INDIANA

Postcard view of the Indiana plant.

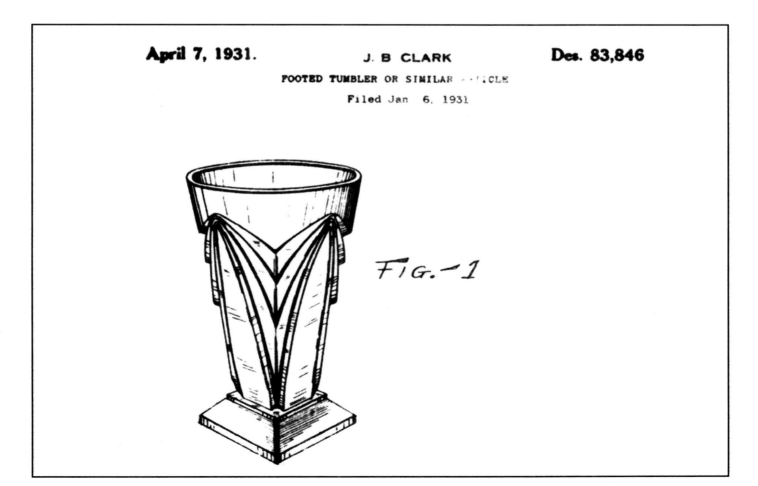

April 7, 1931.   J. B CLARK   Des. 83,846

FOOTED TUMBLER OR SIMILAR ARTICLE

Filed Jan 6. 1931

FIG.-1

JEANNETTE GLASS COMPANY
JEANNETTE, PENNSYLVANIA

CABLE ADDRESS "JNETGLASCO" A B C CODE 5TH EDITION

JEANNETTE GLASS COMPANY

PRESSED AND BLOWN GLASSWARE
"PRIVATE MOLDS OUR SPECIALTY"

MACHINE MADE JARS
AND BOTTLES

NEW YORK OFFICE
2 BARCLAY STREET
PHONE
7045 BARCLAY.

JEANNETTE, PENN'A. Nov. 18th, 1921.

The Jeannette Glass Company was founded in mid-1898, probably as a successor to the Jeannette Bottle Works. By 1918, the firm was installing a producer gas system and listing its products as follows: "vault lights, prism tile, packers' ware, and novelties" (*National Glass Budget*, March 16, 1918).

In 1927-28, the factory was completely outfitted with new automatic glassmaking machinery. The February 20, 1928, issue of *China, Glass and Lamps* had the story:

"One of the most talked of and outstanding lines at the recent Pittsburgh Exhibit was the new colored ware shown by the Jeannette Glass Co., of Jeannette, Pa. This ware is made entirely by the automatic machine and is therefore uniform, both as to shape and color, and is furnished in the two popular colors, namely, pink and green. This glassware is made in continuous tanks and has been finished, not by the hand process, but by the use of especially built polishing and glazing machinery. The items shown included a 21-piece tea set, a 27-piece bridge set and other popular items for tableware use and kitchen ware, which included practically every item furnished in glass for this purpose.

The tea and bridge sets shown were of a very distinctive design, the pattern being a hexagon shaped optic. This optic is very delicate and reflects the color in the glass beautifully. The company has given the name of "Hex-Optic" to this design, which has been carried out in water sets, berry sets and mixing bowl sets besides the tea and bridge sets.

Another item of general interest was the machine made salad plate. There were three designs shown including one plain salad plate for use in the decorating trade. Being automatically made these plates are uniform and can be stacked to a height of six feet or more if necessary. This is a great advantage to the decorating trade and also to the department store buyers, because lack of space in various glass departments make it necessary to stack plates and if they are not uniform it not only takes more room but also shows the irregularity of the plate as soon as the customer sees the stack.

In bringing out this new line of ware the Jeannette Glass Co. was the first, to our knowledge, to make pink glass automatically in a continuous tank as it was also the first to make green glass in the same manner. In order to achieve these results the company necessarily had to do quite a little experimenting, and perhaps it would be of interest to our readers to know that first of all it was necessary to build two especially designed continuous tanks.

The company at present has melting equipment to turn out 50 tons of glass daily and ample shipping facilities to take care of this production. In order to centralize its efforts on machine production the Jeannette Glass Co. has discontinued the manufacture of all hand finished ware and the only hand ware now made is for the various private mould items and jugs for water sets."

The Jeannette plant continued to thrive. In the 1930s, two opaque colors, Jadeite (opaque green) and Delfite (opaque blue) were introduced. Many of the key "Adam to Windsor" Depression Era pattern lines were produced by Jeannette, and readers can learn much about them from Weatherman's books.

No. 2125½
Fruit Tray
Packed 2 dozen in bbl.
Shipping weight 90 lbs.

No. 5108
Candy Jar
Plain or cut
Packed 6 dozen in bbl.
Shipping weight 120 lbs.

No. 2125
Sandwich Tray
Packed 2 dozen in bbl.
Shipping weight 90 lbs.

CABLE ADDRESS "JNETGLASCO" A B C CODE 5TH EDITION

JEANNETTE GLASS COMPANY

PRESSED AND BLOWN GLASSWARE

"PRIVATE MOLDS OUR SPECIALTY"

NEW YORK OFFICE
200 5TH AVENUE

CHICAGO OFFICE
17 NO. WABASH AVE.

FLINTEX
REG. U.S. PAT. OFFICE

JEANNETTE, PENN'A. February 19th, 1924.

ASH TRAYS
CANDY JARS
BOWLS
CANDLESTICKS
CASTER CUPS
DISPLAY FIXTURES
KITCHEN WARE
MIXING BOWLS
NAPPIES
OFFICE SUPPLIES
SHERBERTS
COMPORTS
TUMBLERS
WATER SETS
ICE TEA SETS
HOUSEHOLD SETS
SUGAR AND CREAM SETS
CHEESE AND CRACKER SETS
CUT GLASSWARE
ITEMS FOR CUTTING TRADE
COLORED WARE
AUTO LENSES
SPECIALTIES
CONSOLE SETS
CANDLESTICKS
TOBACCO JARS
BUFFET SETS
AUTOMOBILE VASES

National Assn. Mfg. Pressed & Blown Glassware,
316 House Bldg.,
Pittsburgh, Pa.

Black Glass

Att: Mr. Chas. E. Voitle

Gentlemen:

The shop making our Black Glass Bases are claiming pay for all lehr cracked ware. Will you kindly advise us whether or not this would come under the list as Opal Glass.

Thanking you for your prompt attention, we are

Yours very truly,
JEANNETTE GLASS COMPANY

Frank Smith

CS:M

By:

QUOTATIONS SUBJECT TO CHANGE WITHOUT NOTICE
ALL AGREEMENTS CONTINGENT UPON STRIKES ACCIDENTS AND OTHER DELAYS BEYOND OUR CONTROL.

X-41 Amber Console Set

Consisting of:

   1—5050 Bowl
   2—5201 Candlesticks
   Packed 30 sets to barrel
   Shipping weight 130 lbs.

X-23 Amber Buffet Set

Consisting of:

   1—Bowl No. 5186
   2—Candlesticks No. 5179
   1—Black Base
   Packed 14 sets to barrel
   Shipping weight 130 lbs.

X-30 Amber Buffet Set

Consisting of:

   1—Bowl No. 5164
   2—Candlesticks No. 5198
   1—Black Base
   Packed 15 sets to a barrel
   Shipping weight 115 lbs.

X-31 Amber Buffet Set

Consisting of:

   1—Bowl No. 5215
   2—Candlesticks No. 5201
   Packed 15 sets to a barrel
   Shipping weight 105 lbs.

D. C. JENKINS GLASS COMPANY
KOKOMO AND ARCADIA, INDIANA

This organization began in 1900-1901 when D. C. Jenkins, Jr., and other members of his family formed the Kokomo Glass Manufacturing Company. Previously, they had been associated with the Indiana Tumbler and Goblet Company at nearby Greentown, Indiana, but they left this firm shortly after it was absorbed by the National Glass Company combine.

The plant burned in September,1905, but, with the help of the Kokomo Improvement Association, it was rebuilt and resumed operations in 1906 as the D. C. Jenkins Glass Co. About the time of World War I, another plant was established about 25 miles away at Arcadia, Indiana. The latter plant featured automatic machinery for most of its production, although glass was also made by hand shops there.

Information is scant about Jenkins products, although one c. 1930 catalog survives (this was reprinted in 1984 by the National Greentown Glass Association). The January 23, 1922, issue of *China, Glass and Lamps* mentioned the Jenkins' "new line of figured pressed tableware," but provided little description for it or the No. 921 line, "a near Colonial pattern."

When D. C. Jenkins, Jr., died in August, 1930, his sons Addison and Howard continued to run the organization. Howard had been sales manager for a number of years, and Addison was secretary-treasurer. Despite their experience and enthusiasm, however, the Jenkins firm did not survive the 1930s.

Sandwich Tray
470—10½ in. Plain
471—10½ in. Optic

Note the unusual handle on this Jenkins sandwich tray.

Postcard views of Jenkins plants in Kokomo and Arcadia, c. 1922.

D. C. JENKINS GLASS COMPANY, KOKOMO, IND.

D.C.JENKINS, PRESIDENT.

HOWARD C. JENKINS, SALES MGR.

ADDISON JENKINS, SEC'Y & TREAS.

D.C. JENKINS GLASS COMPANY

MANUFACTURERS OF
PRESSED AND BLOWN GLASSWARE

Kokomo, Ind.

May 29, 1922.

| 980 9 oz. | 980 12 oz. | 980—80 oz. | 981 9 oz. | 981 12 oz. | 981—80 oz. | 982 9 oz. | 982 12 oz. | 982—80 oz. |

| 983 9 oz. | 983 12 oz. | 983—80 oz. | 984 9 oz. | 984 12 oz. | 984—80 oz. | 985 9 oz. | 985 12 oz. | 985—80 oz. |

| 980—80 oz. | 981—80 oz. | 982—80 oz. | 983—80 oz. | 984—80 oz. | 985—80 oz. |

LANCASTER GLASS COMPANY
LANCASTER, OHIO

CODES
A.B.C. FIFTH EDITION
WESTERN UNION
TEL. ADDRESS "LANGLAS"

I.J. COLLINS, PRESIDENT   THOMAS C. FULTON, SECY. & TREAS.

THE LANCASTER GLASS COMPANY

MANUFACTURERS OF
HIGH GRADE TABLE GLASSWARE
SPECIALTIES - NOVELTIES
PLAIN AND DECORATED

LANCASTER, OHIO

December 10th 1932

Ground was broken for this new plant in the summer of 1908. Lucien B. Martin and his son, L. Philip Martin, both of whom had been associated with the nearby Hocking Glass Company, were among the founders of the Lancaster Glass Co. By early 1909, the Lancaster was showing a line of vases in "Crystal, Iridescent, Lustre and Ruby" (*China, Glass and Lamps*, January 9, 1909) as well as tableware lines called Orizaba and Tokay Grape.

In the late teens, the Lancaster Glass Company produced a line of animal and other novelties, most of which have been entirely undocumented until this book.

Lustre ware was being advertised in the spring of 1921, and the colors were described as "a delicate ruby, [a] soft orange hue, and a fascinating canary yellow" (*China, Glass and Lamps*, April 14, 1921). No. 75, a plain colonial line, was on the market later that same year, and these articles were offered: flower bowls, salad plates, sandwich and nut trays, cheese and cracker sets, console sets, bud vases and mayonnaise sets (*Crockery and Glass Journal*, August 7, 1921). A full-page advertisement in *Pottery, Glass and Brass Salesman* (April 6,

(Text continued on page 181)

No. 88—Sandwich Tray

88—5" H. F. Bon Bon & Cover
Packs 4½ dozen to barrel
Weight, 125 lbs.

88—5" L. F. Bon Bon & Cover
Packs 6 dozen to barrel
Weight, 135 lbs.

85—Covered Bon Bon
Packs 5½ dozen to barrel
Weight, 125 lbs.

**Note the various shapes
of these bon bon or candy jars.**

177

NOVELTIES THAT SELL!!

Here's some of our live wire trade winners.   Don't fail to see our latest offerings in Room 706, Fort Pitt Hotel, including "Bingo," "Bathing Girl" and "Eagle."

THEY ARE IN MARTIAL ARRAY

LIFELIKE REPRODUCTION OF WILD AND DOMESTICATED ANIMALS AND BIRDS.

See Our **TABLEWARE** and Lines of Vases.

LANCASTER GLASS CO.

Lancaster, Ohio

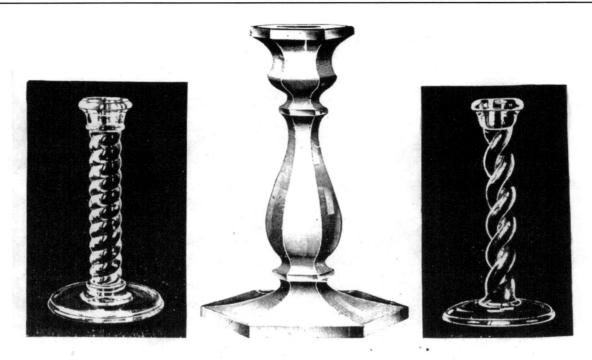

Lancaster Glass Company

"CANDLESTICKMAKERS"

LANCASTER, OHIO

Write for Complete Information and Price List

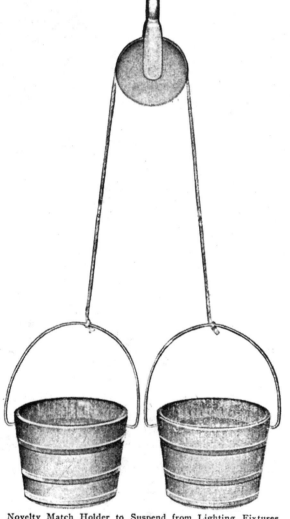

1922) showed six different candlesticks.

The No. 88 sandwich tray was first on the market in early 1923, and an ad in *China, Glass and Lamps* (February 12, 1923) made clear that it was intended for embellishment by "light cutters and decorators" and could be had in either "cold colors or fired colors." This item proved quite popular, and it was still featured in ads many months later (*Pottery, Glass and Brass Salesman*, July 31, 1924). Large assortments of decorated candy jars (78 for $100, wholesale!) were offered in the fall of 1925; these were described as "carefully decorated in four colors—red, canary, green, and blue, with black lines and bands, overlaid with gold (*Crockery and Glass Journal*, October 8, 1925).

In the mid-1920s, several firms—Lancaster Glass Company, Hocking Glass Company, National Lens and Glass Company, Standard Glass Company, and the Steubenville, Ohio, plant of the Gill Bros. Company—were marketing their wares through the Hocking Glass Sales Corporation's newly furnished showroom in New York City at 129-313 Fifth Avenue. The "Collins group," headed by Isaac "Ike" Collins of the Hocking Glass Company controlled all of these firms.

LIBERTY WORKS
EGG HARBOR, NEW JERSEY

According to a retrospective article in *Pottery, Glass and Brass Salesman* (March 29, 1928), this plant began operations as the Liberty Cut Glass Works in 1902. Under the leadership of John E. Marsden, formerly of the Quaker City Cut Glass Company in Philadelphia, the Liberty plant sold heavy cut glass produced from blanks manufactured by other firms. Marsden had established retail outlets for the Liberty's cut glass in many department stores. Ads showing Liberty's cut glass appeared in trade journals such as *Pottery, Glass and Brass Salesman*, especially during 1914.

In the fall of 1925, the Liberty Works, as it was then called, erected a $100,000 addition to its facility. This new construction included a pot furnace, and the Liberty began to make glass about September, 1925. A lengthy article in one of the glass trade publications mentioned "a lavish display of attractive new samples" at the company representative's New York City showroom and went on to offer these intriguing details about the Liberty's colors and specific products:

"One interesting number is a popular priced refreshment set consisting of a covered jug and six glasses. These are in optic, solid colors as well [as] innovation crackled effect in crystal and colors. Green and amber are the colors used as well as iridescent lustre and "Frostina," a frosted effect slightly tinted shading lighter from base to top. There is also another group banded with color at base and collar and with colored cover. Salad plates, to meet the popular demand, are in round and octagonal shape. They are in green, amber and lustre, with cuttings, in solid colors with tiny black bands also with gold band and gold hair line. These are simple yet effective. A general line of fancy table and decorative ware includes bowls, comports, crackers and cheese, candy boxes, etc. These are charmingly decorated with bands and cuttings. Some are in solid colors with gold bands, some with wide black bands with white gold festoon decoration and white gold edge. There are also several numbers in solid colors with the same delicate graceful festooning in black. The colors are soft tones of green and yellow, and vivid tangerine."

In June, 1926—just ten months after beginning to make glass—the Liberty works suffered a disastrous fire. Marsden decided to rebuild the plant, however, and it re-opened in February, 1927. There were several small continuous tank furnaces, and *Pottery, Glass and Brass Salesman* (March 29, 1928) explained that one tank was devoted to "rose color" glass and the other to green.

On August 3, 1926, Edward Meltzer secured a design patent (#70,772), which was assigned to the Liberty Works. This was known as Bamboo Optic, and ads in *Pottery, Glass and Brass Salesman* during 1928 mentioned that it was available in two colors, rose (also called pink) and green.

(Text continued on page 185)

Liberty Cut Glass Works, Egg Harbor City, N. J.

Postcard view of the Liberty plant, c. 1915.

LIGHT CUT TABLE CENTER SET

To Retail at $1.95 Per Set

Another "Liberty" accomplishment of live salable merchandise for profitable retailing.

This set consists of a fifteen-inch bowl and a pair of low candle-holders in a dainty light cut border treatment.

SALESROOM: NEW YORK, 10 WEST 23rd STREET—CHARLES L. WISE, MANAGER

Chicago	Boston	San Francisco	Philadelphia, Baltimore, Washington
E. M. MEDER CO.	PARK E. QUINN	MARSH & KIDD	J. LAWRENCE CUMMINS
17 North Wabash Avenue	99 Bedford Street	617 Mission Street	

LIGHT CUT TABLE CENTER SET

To Retail At $1.95 Per Set

Another "Liberty" accomplishment of live salable merchandise for profitable retailing.

This set consists of a fifteen-inch bowl and a pair of low candle-holders in a dainty light cut border treatment.

SALESROOM: NEW YORK, 10 WEST 23rd STREET—CHARLES L. WISE, MANAGER

Chicago	Boston	San Francisco
E. M. MEDER CO.	PARK E. QUINN	MARSH & KIDD
17 North Wabash Avenue	99 Bedford Street	617 Mission Street

Philadelphia, Baltimore, Washington	Southeast	Southwest
J. LAWRENCE CUMMINS	C. A. BRADSHAW	UNITED IMPORT & EXPORT CORP.
	Shreveport, La.	El Paso, Texas

BAMBOO OPTIC

Illustrated is our 21-piece luncheon set consisting of six cups, six saucers, six luncheon plates, sugar and cream and a 11-inch cake plate. The charm of the bamboo optic pattern in which they are shown will be readily seen. The fact should also be noted that the ware is very light in weight, yet not too fragile, being well made and annealed. Obtainable in rose or green glass. Shorter sets can be made up, including a 12-piece bridge set, consisting of four cups and saucers and four plates, or a 13-inch bridge set by adding the cake. The values are remarkable. Sets can be retailed as low as $1.95 for some combinations. Write us for prices and terms.

LIBERTY WORKS REPRESENTATIVES:

EGG HARBOR, N.J.

New York
CHARLES L. WISE
10 West 23rd Street

Philadelphia, Baltimore, Washington
J. LAWRENCE CUMMINS

Chicago
E. M. MEDER
17 North Wabash Avenue

Southeast
C. A. BRADSHAW
Shreveport, La.

Boston
PARKE QUINN
99 Bedford Street

Pennsylvania and New York States
THOMAS B. CANNON

San Francisco
MARSH & KIDD
617 Mission Street

Southwest
UNITED IMPORT & EXPORT CORP.
El Paso, Texas

Octagon Optic (somewhat similar to the Cambridge Glass Company's Decagon line) was advertised in *Pottery, Glass and Brass Salesman* in 1929, and both rose and green were mentioned.

A Liberty salad set (called "Robin" by Weatherman) was advertised in *Pottery, Glass and Brass Salesman* (February 6, 1930), and Liberty's American Pioneer line, described as "colonial hobnail and flute design," appeared in the same publication (March 5, 1931)

Although Weatherman suggests that Liberty made glass in "almost every color known," the ads shown by Weatherman mention only crystal, emerald/green and pink/rose. A fire in 1932 marked the demise of this plant.

Aug. 3, 1926.   Des. 70,772

E. MELTZER
GLASS JUG OR SIMILAR ARTICLE
Filed May 21, 1926

Patent drawing and ads for various Liberty products.

McKee Glass Company
Jeannette, Pennsylvania

This paragraph—from a January, 1915, glass industry trade journal—provides an apt history of the town of Jeannette and the crown jewel of its industry:

"The founding of this town twenty-six years ago was appropriately celebrated on New Year's Day. In 1888 Jeannette was a vast sand lot and the McKee Glass Company was one of the first industries to be driven from Pittsburgh by exorbitant taxation. David Carle, who went from the South Side with H. Sellers McKee to what is now the thrifty little city, directed the affairs of the celebration. Fifteen years ago Mr. McKee disposed of his interests in Jeannette and has since resided in New York. He was the guest of honor and was royally entertained. The city was named after Mrs. McKee."

In late 1922, McKee was advertising its heat-resistant patented GlasBake ware as well as other products such as console sets and a handled sandwich tray in two new satin finish colors, "Jap Blue and Jade Yellow" (*Pottery, Glass and Brass Salesman*, December 14, 1922). The "Rock Crystal" was made in these colors and continued as a McKee staple for some time.

The McKee firm continued to introduce new products, even during the depths of the Depression Era. In 1933, for example, Jade Green was prominent, and French Ivory made its debut in the Laurel tableware set.

In 1938, McKee developed Patio

kitchenware, and one trade journal described the colors as "rich yellow, orange, green and blue, sold most popularly in combinations ..."

McKee glass in a premium catalog.

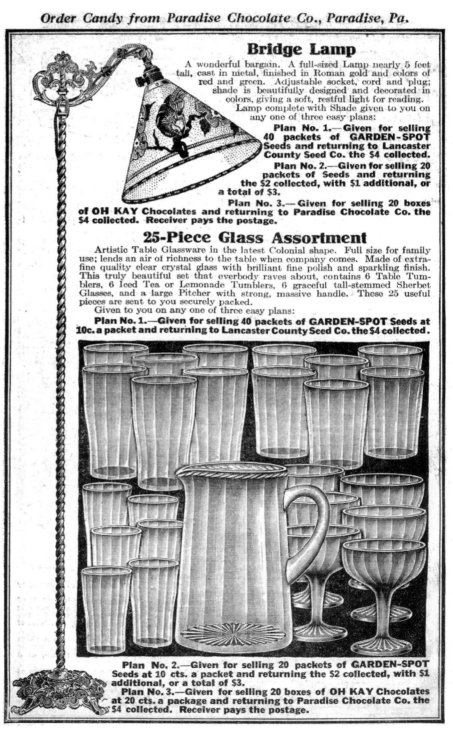

Order Candy from Paradise Chocolate Co., Paradise, Pa.

Bridge Lamp

A wonderful bargain. A full-sized Lamp nearly 5 feet tall, cast in metal, finished in Roman gold and colors of red and green. Adjustable socket, cord and plug; shade is beautifully designed and decorated in colors, giving a soft, restful light for reading. Lamp complete with Shade given to you on any one of three easy plans:

Plan No. 1.—Given for selling 40 packets of GARDEN-SPOT Seeds and returning to Lancaster County Seed Co. the $4 collected.

Plan No. 2.—Given for selling 20 packets of Seeds and returning the $2 collected, with $1 additional, or a total of $3.

Plan No. 3.— Given for selling 20 boxes of OH KAY Chocolates and returning to Paradise Chocolate Co. the $4 collected. Receiver pays the postage.

25-Piece Glass Assortment

Artistic Table Glassware in the latest Colonial shape. Full size for family use; lends an air of richness to the table when company comes. Made of extra-fine quality clear crystal glass with brilliant fine polish and sparkling finish. This truly beautiful set that everbody raves about, contains 6 Table Tumblers, 6 Iced Tea or Lemonade Tumblers, 6 graceful tall-stemmed Sherbet Glasses, and a large Pitcher with strong, massive handle. These 25 useful pieces are sent to you securely packed.

Given to you on any one of three easy plans:

Plan No. 1.—Given for selling 40 packets of GARDEN-SPOT Seeds at 10c. a packet and returning to Lancaster County Seed Co. the $4 collected.

Plan No. 2.—Given for selling 20 packets of GARDEN-SPOT Seeds at 10 cts. a packet and returning the $2 collected, with $1 additional, or a total of $3.

Plan No. 3.—Given for selling 20 boxes of OH KAY Chocolates at 20 cts. a package and returning to Paradise Chocolate Co. the $4 collected. Receiver pays the postage.

McKee glass in pink with elaborate decoration was shown in a premium catalog.

ROSE PINK GLASSWARE
Manufactured by McKee Glass Company, Jeannette, Pa.
Beautifully Cut in Diamond Lattice and Floral Design

No.	Coupons
1298—Handled Lunch Plate. Diameter 11 inches...................................	625
1299—Handled Nut Bowl. Diameter 8½ inches	625
1300—Candy Jar. Capacity 1 pound..........	625
1301—Fruit Bowl. Diameter 9 inches..........	625
5463—Covered Nappy. Bowl divided into three sections. Diameter 7 inches................	700

No.	Coupons
5461—Vase. Height 10 inches...............	725
5464—Center Piece. (Bowl) Diameter 10 inches	725
5460—Sugar and Creamer...................	825
1302—Mayonnaise Bowl, Plate and Ladle....	875
5462—Cheese and Cracker Dish. Diameter 11 inches....................................	1000
5465—Candlesticks. One pair. Height 2⅛ inches. Diameter 4½ inches...............	1000

DO NOT ENCLOSE WRITTEN MATTER IN A PACKAGE SENT BY THIRD OR FOURTH CLASS MAIL. IT IS A VIOLATION OF THE POSTAL LAWS.

McKee covered dish from a 1935 patent.

SEE THE NEW ADDITIONS TO OUR REFRESHMENT SETS, GLASBAKE, CUT GLASS AND COLORED WARE LINES AT THE PITTSBURGH CROCKERY AND GLASS SHOW.

FORT PITT HOTEL

ROOMS 743 AND 797

JANUARY 10th TO 27th, 1927

We manufacture Tableware, Pressed Tumblers and Stemware, Lamps, Soda Fountain Ware, Stationers' Glassware, Cut Glass, Colored Light Cut Glass, Glasbake Cooking Ware, Automobile, Marine and Signal Lenses and Semaphores, Sanitary Coolers, Art Glass Clocks, Colored Glassware, Hotel Supply Ware, Steam Table Inserts, Special Moulds, etc.

McKEE GLASS CO.

Established 1853

JEANNETTE, PA., U. S. A.

FALL AND HOLIDAY LINES

"BETTY JANE" TOY COOKING GLASS SET
(Copyright)

"BETTY JANE" SET
(Copyright)

Glasbake Guaranteed Cooking Ware

Any little Lady will appreciate this gift.

This set has all the features of the regular size Glasbake utensils, including the "Heat-Quick" corrugated bottom.

Each set consists of the following pieces:

1— ¼ Quart Covered Casserole
1—4½ Inch Bread Pan
1—5 Inch Pie Plate
2—3 Ounce Round Bakers

Every set packed in a fancy seven colored lithographed display box.

Sets can be furnished in either the plain or fluted pattern.

COVERED MEAT LOAF DISH

GLASBAKE COOKING WARE

The lines of Glasbake Cooking Ware are now complete having added many new items to the regular staple line and also contain many exclusive pieces such as the Tube Cake Pan and Muffin Pans.

Each piece of GLASBAKE Ware is guaranteed not to break from oven use and has the special advantage of the "Heat-Quick" bottom, another exclusive feature.

Two patterns of GLASBAKE Ware, the plain and the fluted (Patented) are manufactured by us.

TWO PIECE BRIDGE SET

COLORED GIFTWARES
—Solid Colors—

We manufacture complete lines of Colored giftwares both in transparent and satin finish colors that contain all the staple items that are selling in this class of goods. Our colors are Blue, Canary, Amber, Green and Amethyst.

Have you seen our line of Innovation Crackled Ware (Patented) in crystal and colors that features such items as Ice Tea Sets, Water Sets, Grape Juice Sets, Beverage Sets, Console Sets, Handled Lunch Plates, Cheese and Cracker Sets, etc?

Write for Illustrations and Quotations

McKEE GLASS COMPANY

Established 1853   JEANNETTE, PA., U. S. A.

NEW CUMBERLAND GLASS COMPANY
NEW CUMBERLAND, WEST VIRGINIA

This enterprise should not be confused with the Cumberland Glass Co. of Cumberland, Maryland. Unfortunately, very little is known about the New Cumberland concern, but there is one advertisement which shows a handled sandwich tray and alludes to an interesting variety of colors.

On February 17, 1921, *China, Glass and Lamps* reported that "The plant of the New Cumberland Glass Co., at New Cumberland, W. Va., is idle. Windows have been boarded and there is no outward sign as to when fires will again be lighted." Some months later (December 13, 1923), however, *Pottery, Glass and Brass Salesman* noted that "The new plant of the New Cumberland Glass Co., of New Cumberland, WV, will start operations some time this month. The structure is three times as large as the old plant destroyed by fire several months ago."

A report in *Crockery and Glass Journal* (January, 19, 1925) offers a little insight into the company's products and provides a bit of history: "A new line of decorated novelties is now being produced at the plant of the New Cumberland Glass Co., at New Cumberland, WV, of which W. G. Edmunds is in charge. The initial plant of the company was destroyed by fire several years ago, and after a reorganization of the company was completed, a new larger factory was erected and placed in operation."

Five years later, the plant may have been out of business for good: "According to rumors which emanate from Cumberland, W. Va., Pittsburgh capital is said to be interested in the purchase and operation of the plant of the old New Cumberland Glass Company, which has been idle ..." (*Pottery, Glass and Brass Salesman*, February 20, 1930).

OUR SPECIAL ANNOUNCEMENT

Our New Lines of Special Glassware will be shown at the Glass Manufacturers Exhibit, from Jan. 5th., to 24th., 1925, at Hotel Henry, Fifth Avenue, Pittsburgh, Pa. Rooms 11 and 15, Parlor Floor.

You are invited to call and look over what we have to offer in new items for the next year.

Lines of Glassware will be shown made from Crystal, Colored Glass, Amber, Blue, Black, Green, Canary, Brown, etc. Special Pearl, Brown and Green Agate Ware will be shown for the first time. Also light cut ware, decorated and etched glassware will be shown.

SALES WILL BE IN CHARGE OF—
Mr. W. G. Edmonds, Gen. Mgr.   Mr. Lee O. Smith, Representative.
Also Factory Representatives.

NEW CUMBERLAND GLASS COMPANY
NEW CUMBERLAND, WEST VA.

This is one of the few ads for the new Cumberland firm; note the extensive listing of colors.

New Martinsville Glass Company
New Martinsville, West Virginia

In late 1900, glassmen Mark Douglass and George Matheny established a plant in New Martinsville (Wetzel County) West Virginia. The firm's immediate successor, the Viking Glass Company, closed in the mid-1980s. From the early 1900s through WWI, the New Martinsville plant introduced several new patterns each year, ranging from intricate imitation cut glass motifs (often with gold decoration and ruby stain) to plain colonial-style lines.

Colored glass was in vogue during the 1920s, and the New Martinsville firm kept pace. Console sets in colored glass were decorated with hand-painted enamel or cuttings. These glass colors were used from 1922-26 for console sets, vanity sets, smokers articles and other items: amber, blue, green, and amethyst. A few articles occur in black glass, and, in May, 1926, a pale pink color color called Peach Melba was introduced. Some New Martinsville pieces were marked with a distinctive

FOUR PIECE VANITY SET
in crystal, and crystal with jade
or bright green covers and stoppers.
These retail at $1 each
— great promotional items!

trademark—a block M with a vertical line at the middle which creates the appearance of an N superimposed upon the M.

When Robert McEldowney took over as general manager in late 1926, the firm's reputation for colored ware was well-established. McEldowney registered designs for New Martinsville's No. 33 Modernistic line in 1928. The Art Deco look is quite distinctive.

In early 1930, New Martinsville introduced a new line, No. 34. Intended as a complete luncheon set, it encompassed handled sandwich tray, plates, juice glasses and tumblers (6 oz. and 9 oz.), cups and saucers, creamer and sugar, and a small comport. Another luncheon set made in the early 1930s was No. 35, called Fancy Squares today. Vanity sets (consisting of a powder box with two perfume bottles on a tray) were also an integral part of New Martinsville's production

Just as the plant fell on financial hard times in the early 1930s, general manager Ira Clarke developed the No. 37 line, which collectors today call Moondrops. Numerous ads appeared in trade publications, and No. 37 was made in amber, amethyst, black, dark blue and light blue, ruby and two shades of transparent green as well as a cloudy crystal called "smoke" by collectors. Opaque jade green, black and smoke are hard to find, but ruby and Ritz Blue (cobalt blue) seem to be most popular. The number of articles available in No. 37 (Moondrops) is impressive indeed.

Although No. 37 probably kept the factory from closing there were other important lines. No. 42 Radiance was made for years as were two other two new pattern lines, No. 44 (or 4400) and No. 45 (or 4500) Janice line. Both were in production throughout the early 1940s, and the moulds remained when the New Martinsville firm was reorganized as the Viking Glass Company in 1944.

For more information, readers should consult *New Martinsville Glass, 1900-1944* (Marietta: Antique Publications, 1994).

No. 10/2
Console
Set

Brighten Up Your Stock!
Jazz Up Your Sales!

Here is an entirely new idea: Glass Comport candlesticks for the Large Whip Candles. Made in the beautiful colors of the vogue:

*Amber, Green, Blue or
Amethyst and Crystal*

They can also be had in Most Attractive Black Decorations

Packed 1½ dozen to a barrel

THE NEW MARTINSVILLE GLASS CO.
New Martinsville, W. Va.

———

Ira M. Clark, Gen. Mgr.

H. NORTHWOOD AND COMPANY
WHEELING, WEST VIRGINIA

H. Northwood and Co. was the last American glass concern to benefit from the talent and genius of Harry Northwood. An English immigrant who came to the United States in 1881, he was a glass etcher at Hobbs-Brockunier in Wheeling before joining the La Belle Glass Co. in nearby Bridgeport, Ohio, in 1884. He soon became the driving force at La Belle, where he was responsible for both glass chemistry and product design.

When the La Belle was destroyed by fire in 1887, its key investors rallied around Harry Northwood and, in 1888, established the Northwood Glass Company at Martins Ferry, Ohio, a short distance above Bridgeport on the Ohio River. The plant's capacity was small, however, and flood damage was frequent, so the enterprise moved itself to Ellwood City, Pennsylvania, in 1892. Backed by Northwood's wealthy uncle Thomas Dugan , this venture lasted just three years before Northwood and his brother Carl went to Indiana, Pa., to revive a glass plant there.

The brothers returned to England briefly around the turn of the century after the Indiana plant was purchased by the National Glass Company combine and they became London-based sales agents for this concern. The National soon fell on financial hard times, so they decided to return to the United States. They were attracted to Wheeling, where the local Board of Trade helped finance a renovation of the old Hobbs-Brockunier plant in which Harry had begun his career.

The Northwood firm made iridescent ware from 1908 through 1915, and Harry held several patents for glass designs and fixtures, including lighting goods which were instrumental in the firm's success around WWI. Carl Northwood passed away in January, 1918, and Harry died in February, 1919.

Without Harry and Carl at the helm, the Northwood plant soon fell into difficulties. Nonetheless, the company managed by James Haden was eager to compete, and it introduced new products and colors during the first half of the 1920s.

Blue Iris and Topaz Iris were followed by opaque Jade Blue in 1921 and by the distinctive Russet in 1922. Jade Green was next in 1923-24. The final Northwood colors were a rich opaque red called Chinese Coral and a deep transparent amber dubbed Rosita Amber. Operations began to wind down during the fall of 1925, and the plant was closed in December of that year.

For more information on Northwood glass, consult *Harry Northwood: The Wheeling Years, 1901-1925* (Marietta: Antique Publications, 1991).

Topaz Irridescent

Blue Irridescent

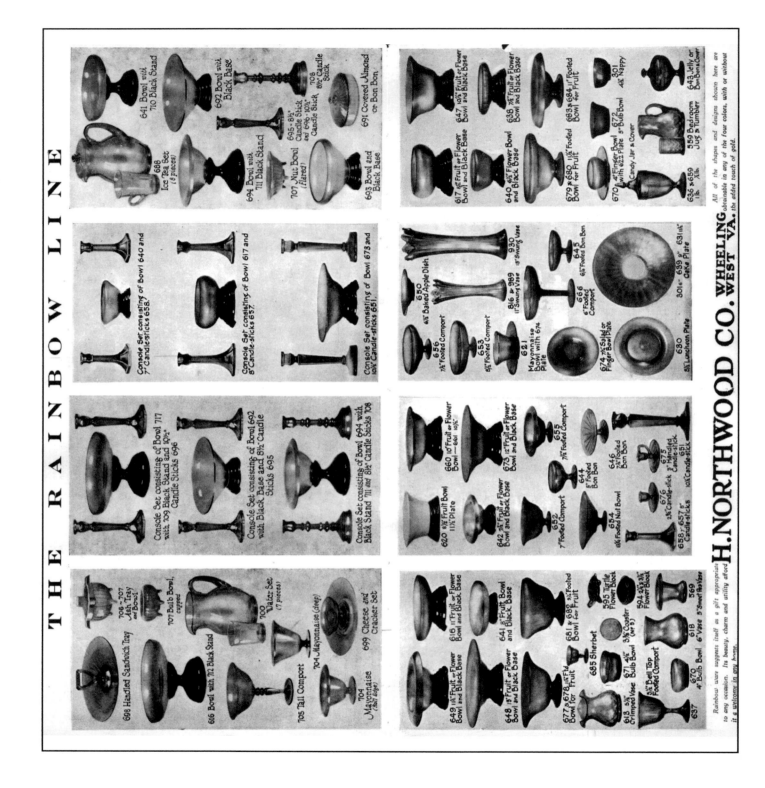

THE RAINBOW LINE

H. NORTHWOOD CO. WHEELING. WEST VA.

PADEN CITY GLASS MANUFACTURING COMPANY
PADEN CITY, WEST VIRGINIA

DAVID FISHER, PRES. AND GEN. MGR.
W. J. McCOY, VICE PRESIDENT

J. J. McKAY,
SECRETARY AND TREASURER

PADEN CITY GLASS MANUFACTURING CO.

MANUFACTURERS OF

PRESSED AND BLOWN GLASSWARE---PLAIN, CUT, DECORATED AND ETCHED

HOTEL AND SODA FOUNTAIN SUPPLIES
GOBLETS AND TUMBLERS, LAMPS AND STATIONERS' GLASSWARE

SPECIAL MOULDS

PADEN CITY, WEST VA.

This enterprise began in April, 1916, when David Fisher (who was then associated with the nearby New Martinsville Glass Manufacturing Company) signed a contract with a committee seeking to build a new glass tableware plant at Paden City, a small town which straddles the border of Wetzel and Tyler counties about five miles south of New Martinsville. Many New Martinsville glassworkers, especially those who were particularly adept pressers or finishers, found employment at Paden City when work was slack in New Martinsville or vice-versa.

David Fisher headed the Paden City Glass Manufacturing Company until his death on May 21, 1933. His son Samuel succeeded him, and Robert McEldowney left the New Martinsville Glass Manufacturing Company to join the Paden City plant. Both Samuel Fisher and Robert McEldowney were associated with the Paden City firm until it closed in the fall of 1951. Many Paden City products bear strong resemblances to glassware made at New Martinsville. Weatherman shows many products, but, unfortunately, she often deleted the original pattern names and numbers.

At Paden City, new pattern lines were introduced regularly. Between 1919 and 1937, for instance, these were advertised: No. 202 (1919); No. 204 (1920); No. 206 (1922); No. 209 (1923); No. 207 (1924); No. 700 (c. 1925); No. 701 (c. 1926); No. 191, No. 191 1/2 and No. 192 (1927); No. 210 (c. 1928-29); No. 881 (1932); No. 69 Georgian (1934); No. 90 Chavalier (1935); No. 220 (1937). Collectors generally refer to Paden City glass using fanciful pattern names such as Penny and Crow's Foot, however.

The colors produced at Paden City were similar to those made at New Martinsville and many other factories. Paden City did have several unique names, such as Cheriglo (pink), Mulberry (amethyst) and Primrose (reddish amber). The mid-1920s seem to be the zenith of Paden City's color production. These other colors are listed from time to time: amber, black or Ebony, blue (both a cobalt hue called Royal Blue and a light blue called either Copen or Neptune), crystal; green, rose (dark pink), ruby and topaz.

In September, 1932, Paden City introduced opal (milk glass) which was called Snow Flake (sometimes written Snowflake). Cocktail sets (consisting of a tall shaker and six tumblers) were offered; these bear a farm scene and the words "Be it ever so humble, there's no place like home."

During the late 1920s and the 1930s, Paden City decorated a good deal of its glassware with cuttings or plate etchings. Among today's collectors, the popular plate etchings have these names: Cupid, Nora Bird, Orchid, Peacock Reverse, and Peacock and Wild Rose. Much research remains to be done on Paden City plate etchings.

The Paden City Glass Manufacturing Company closed in 1951. Quite a few moulds were purchased by the Canton Glass Company of Marion, Indiana, and at least a few were acquired by the Fenton Art Glass Company and the Viking Glass Company. The only study devoted exclusively to this firm, Jerry Barnett's privately printed *Paden City: The Color Company* (1978), is long out of print, but there are many pages of black and white catalog reprints in Weathermans' books.

L. E. SMITH GLASS COMPANY
MT. PLEASANT, PENNSYLVANIA

The L. E. Smith Glass Company celebrated its 90th anniversary in 1997. According to the firm's current catalog, the company began in 1907 when mustard producer Lewis Smith needed containers for his foodstuffs. The company occupied its plant in Mt. Pleasant, Pa., after acquiring it from the then-bankrupt Anchor Glass Company, a bottle maker. A fire in 1913 spelled near disaster, but the plant was rebuilt, and the business of making various containers continued to grow.

In 1920, the Smith organization purchased the Greensburg Glass Company's plant and assets, which included a number of moulds. The Greensburg factory was eventually used to make automobile headlight lenses, but it certainly played a role in Smith's production of tableware and related glass during the 1920s and, perhaps, into the Depression Era as well. Soda fountain articles were an important feature of Smith's output.

These ranged from sundae and soda glasses in various sizes to napkin holders, ash trays and "guaranteed sanitary" sugar pours!

Although the Smith firm is best known today for its production of black glass in the 1920s-1930s, there were many other colors, including amber, amethyst, blue, canary, crystal, green and pink as well as opaque white milk glass. In some of the luncheon sets, customers could choose all black pieces or select a combination of crystal and black (e. g., crystal cups on black saucers, etc.). The scarce covered urns in black glass shown in this book were featured in *Crockery and Glass Journal* for January, 1935.

The Smith firm developed a Moon and Star pattern line decades ago, and this continues to be a popular product. When the Imperial Glass Corp. closed in the 1980s, the Smith organization bought some of its moulds, and quite a few of these are featured in the current Smith catalog.

NO. 1—COOKIE JAR
BLACK GLASS WITH FANCY DECORATION

NO. 3—COOKIE JAR
CAPACITY—NINE POUNDS
BLACK GLASS WITH FANCY DECORATIONS

NO. 4 COOKIE JAR
BLACK GLASS WITH FANCY DECORATION

L. E. SMITH GLASS COMPANY

United States Glass Company
Pittsburgh, Pennsylvania

This organization, formed in 1891, was actually a combine of 15 previously independent plants. From the outset, the U. S. Glass Co. embraced some of the most prestigious glassmaking establishments in nineteenth century America, such as Hobbs (formerly Hobbs-Brockunier) of Wheeling, Challinor-Taylor of Tarentum, and seven important Pittsburgh firms.

The new company tried to achieve economies of scale, and it also hoped to reduce competition and lower wage costs by running with non-union labor. Another goal was to consolidate manufacturing in fewer plants and to have the individual factories specialize in particular kinds of glassware.

In early 1921, a full-page ad in *China, Glass and Lamps* revealed the breadth and depth of the U. S. Glass organization at that time. Factory E was devoted entirely to tumblers, while Factory L focused on lighting globes. Several plants made tableware and could do cutting, but decorating (gold accents and/or handpainting) was concentrated in Factories D and N. Although each plant had its own personality and its own products, all marketing and publicity came through the company headquarters in Pittsburgh.

The United States Glass company marketed a tremendous array of colors and decorative effects between 1920 and 1940, and many of the original names are mentioned in glass industry trade journals. Unfortunately, since publicity notes came from reporters who visited the U. S. Glass Co. headquarters and showroom in Pittsburgh, the descriptions do not always mention the specific factory where the color or decoration was being produced. Furthermore, the accounts are often frustratingly short, simply because the trade press writers assumed that readers had seen (or would soon see) the colors being described!

As early as 1912, the United States Glass Company was making iridescent glass. *Pottery, Glass and Brass Salesman* (January 18, 1912) mentions iridescent ware in "an amber tint" as well as an effect called "mother-of-pearl." The generic name "Aurora" was soon being used to cover the various iridescent colors being made by the United States Glass Company (*Crockery and Glass Journal*, June 8, 1916). "Dark steel grey" and "light steel

grey" were noted, as was "an extra heavy iridescent ruby" (*Pottery, Glass and Brass Salesman*, December 28, 1916). U. S. Glass Co. ads soon listed "Green, Yellow, Claret [and] Blue" as the firm's iridescent colors in February, 1917.

In the fall of 1917, *Pottery, Glass and Brass Salesman* mentioned "Silicalene" glass and said that it was featured in the company's No. 15187 line. Several opaque colors ("pearl blue, coral red and jade green") were noted in a July, 1921, issue of *Crockery and Glass Journal*, and the No. 310 (or 15310) line was illustrated in several trade journals in early 1922 (this line was called Chatham, although the name does not seem to have been used very much).

The terms Aurora Blue, Aurora Canary, and Aurora Crystal [probably in place of "mother-of-pearl"] were also in use (*Crockery and Glass Journal*, January 12, 1922). The opaque colors may have been grouped under the general term "Carrara" or "Cumula," and one trade journal called this "glassware that looks like pottery, a novelty" (*Pottery, Glass and Brass Salesman*, March 9, 1922). "Pomona" and "Autumn" were also mentioned.

Translucent Florentine colors (Mandarin Yellow, Nile Green and Old Rose) debuted in 1922, but Old Rose was apparently dropped after just a few months. An advertisement in the London, England, *Pottery Gazette and Glass Trade Review* (February 1, 1923) mentions these interesting colors: Peacock Blue, Canary Yellow, Raven Black and Peach Blow. In late 1923, the United States Glass company invited buyers to see the firm's catalog, boasting that it offered "25,000 pieces to Choose From!" A few months later, the Pittsburgh showroom at 954 Liberty Avenue was said to have "some 30,000 pieces of glassware ... attractively displayed."

In the mid-1920s, the United States Glass Company published a monthly booklet, "The Glass Outlook," which contained photographs and news about the company's products. The year 1926 brought forth a number of pitchers and ice tea tumblers, particularly in crystal with decorative effects and bases and handles s in a contrasting color such as blue or green, A lustred glassware with "a rather mottled effect" was called Jack Frost (*China, Glass and Lamps*, January

(Text continued on page 201)

WE CONTEND

That we manufacture the best and most complete line of

GLASSWARE

in the country.   Here is the proof:

FACTORY A

SODA FOUNTAIN ITEMS
JUGS
FISH GLOBES
AUTOMOBILE LENS'

FACTORY B

PRESSED TABLEWARE
BIRD BATHS, SEED CUPS
CANDY TRAYS AND JARS
OILS, SALTS AND PEPPERS
LAMPS

FACTORY D

LEAD BLOWN DECORATED WARE
PRESSED DECORATED WARE
DECORATED ASSORTMENTS

FACTORY E

ICE TEAS
HOTEL TUMBLERS
TABLE TUMBLERS

FACTORY F

BERRY BOWLS AND NAPPIES
GRADUATES
BEST QUALITY FANCY DISPLAY JARS
SALVERS
BLANKS FOR CUTTING

FACTORY G

ALTAR WARE, CANDLESTICKS
BITTER BOTTLES
VASES
HIGH GRADE TABLEWARE
FIGURED BLANKS FOR CUTTING
LIME BLANKS FOR CUTTING
BEAUTIFUL LIGHT CUTTINGS

FACTORY K

TUMBLERS
PRESSED STEMWARE
EGGS, SHERBETS, SUNDAES
VASES
TABLEWARE
FURNITURE KNOBS
MURANO (WHITE) WARE
HIGH GRADE LIGHT CUTTINGS

FACTORY N

DECORATED TABLEWARE
DECORATED FISH GLOBES
DECORATED VASES
DECORATED ASSORTMENTS

FACTORY O

LIME BLOWN SHELLS
COMMON AND HOTEL TUMBLERS
CONFECTION AND CIGAR JARS
PROVISION AND UNIVERSAL JARS
TABLEWARE

FACTORY R

FINEST QUALITY LEAD BLOWN
    WARE, PLAIN
HIGHEST GRADE LEAD BLOWN
    WARE BEAUTIFULLY CUT AND
    ETCHED
SUPREME QUALITY WARE

FACTORY U

TABLEWARE AND TABLEWARE AS-
    SORTMENTS
TUMBLERS AND PRESSED STEM-
    WARE
CONDIMENT AND OINTMENT JARS
LAMPS, MOLASSES CANS   -
HIGH GRADE LIGHT CUT WARE

FACTORY L

DEVOTED EXCLUSIVELY TO PRODUC-
    ING THE MOST PRACTICAL AS
    WELL AS BEAUTIFUL LIGHTING
    GLOBES.

What are your needs?   We can supply them.

UNITED STATES GLASS CO. Pittsburgh, Pa.

The world's largest makers of
HOUSEHOLD GLASSWARE *present*
TIFFIN *ware*

The gold Tiffin crest on every piece.

TIFFIN

[*Four pieces of fine crystal in the authentic* Flanders *pattern. See your dealer.*]

Now on display in leading department, housefurnishing, glassware and dining ware stores everywhere.

SEE your dealer's display of TIFFIN today — tableware of lustrous, sparkling glass in crystal and radiant colors . . . individual pieces that add new color, brilliance and decorative interest to any room.

The glassmaker's art is "half as old as time." In Tiffinware, the priceless, almost forgotten practises of the ancients are reborn — plus rare beauty and strength which only modern methods make possible.

Tiffin completely satisfies the modern woman's desire for correct table appointment and tasteful home adornment. Your table set with Tiffinware is in the smartest of fashion. Your tableware is not complete without it. Especially ask to see the Bridge-luncheon set of Tiffin.

Start your set of Tiffinware today, from open stock patterns — as you choose your best silver. The Tiffin crest on every piece.

UNITED STATES GLASS CO.
Pittsburgh, Pa.

The Priscilla — *a smart new one-piece dish for serving breakfast cereals, fruit, desserts and a hundred other uses. In apple green or rose pink — only $2.50 per set of six, at your dealer's.*

Etiquette of Table Glassware—FREE
Every woman should have the new book, by Caroline Duer, Editor of VOGUE'S Book of Etiquette. It's free. Send the coupon.

UNITED STATES GLASS CO.,
Dept. A, So. Ninth St., Pittsburgh, Pa.
   Kindly send me a FREE copy of the new book, "The Hostess and Her Table," by Caroline Duer.

Name . . . .
Address . . . .
City . . . . State . . . .

In using advertisements see page 6

18, 1926). Royal Blue was introduced about this time, as was Mulberry. These colors came in a wide variety of decorative effects. Royal Purple was being marketed in the summer of 1927 (*Crockery and Glass Journal*, August 18, 1927).

By 1929-30, there were others transparent colors: Rose Pink, Apple Green, and Twilight Blue. Opaque black remained popular, however, and one trade journal had this to say about the United States Glass Company's Tiffin plant: "It is a pure black, a real jet, and by reason of the good quality of the metal turned out by the Tiffin plant, has a good deal of depth to it (*Pottery, Glass and Brass Salesman*, February 20, 1930). Shortly thereafter, "Tiffin Ware" was being advertised nationally by the United States Glass Company, and the reputation and the longevity of this particular United States Glass Company plant were assured.

For more information, readers should consult Fred Bickenheuser's series of three *Tiffin Glassmasters* books as well as the recent *Tiffin Glass* by Jerry Gallagher and Leslie Pina). Nonetheless, there is a lot more to learn about the United States Glass Company and its products.

VIKING GLASS COMPANY
NEW MARTINSVILLE, WEST VIRGINIA

This firm succeeded the New Martinsville Glass Company, but the process was complex. The original firm (New Martinsville Glass Manufacturing Company) was in receivership for much of the 1930s, but, just after Ira M. Clarke's leadership had restored a measure of stability, he died suddenly in April, 1937. A court receiver was appointed, and the plant (along with all moulds and fixtures) was sold in mid-1938 to two men associated with the Silver City Glass Company of Meriden, Connecticut.

The plant was reopened as the New Martinsville Glass Company, but, in late 1941, a trade publication revealed that the firm was going to change its name to the Viking Glass Company in keeping with the Swedish-style ware then in production. In fact, the name change was not officially accomplished until the stockholders met in June, 1944. Nonetheless, knowledge of Viking glass is important to those who collect glassware from the 1920s and 1930s, because many earlier New Martinsville moulds were continued in production by Viking.

The Viking Glass Company closed its doors in 1986, but Kenneth Dalzell, who had been an executive at the Fostoria Glass Company in nearby Moundsville, formed Dalzell-Viking Corporation to operate the glass plant in New Martinsville. In April, 1998, the plant ceased production, and its future was uncertain.

VINELAND FLINT GLASS COMPANY
VINELAND, NEW JERSEY

Although this company is well-known for the Durand art glass made there in the mid-1920s, its other products should not go unrecorded. The company began as a producer of glass tubing, flasks and other scientific glassware, and it was eventually absorbed by the Kimble Glass Company, which continued this specialization.

During the 1920s, in addition to the Durand art glass, the Vineland Flint Glass company made the sort of iridescent ware which is called "stretch glass" by collectors today. At least three colors are known--amber, blue and purple. The amber may have had the original name "Old Gold," but this has not yet been verified. The blue was called "Tut Blue," and the purple was dubbed "Wisteria" (Fenton also used this name for its glass of a similar character). These colors were used to make an assortment of candlesticks and console bowls (with black bases).

Some of Vineland's console bowls and candlesticks are quite similar in design to those made by Fenton and Northwood. However, the tall colonial-style candlestick made by Vineland was produced in a three-part mould; Fenton and Northwood colonial-style candlesticks were made in two-part moulds). At first glance, many of the Vineland firm's console bowls also look similar to those made by other companies. Upon closer examination, one will notice differences in the bases and in the shapes themselves, particularly the distinctively crimped bowls.

In his *Stretch in Color* (1971), Berry Wiggins

pictured the undersides of two Vineland bowls in order to show the original paper labels. These labels, reproduced in facsimile below, reveal the original numbers (12 and 15, respectively) for Vineland's Tut Blue and Wisteria colors.

Vineland Flint Glass Works
Vineland, N. J.

No. 12. Tut Blue

Vineland Flint Glass Works
Vineland, N. J.

No. 15. Wisteria

Westmoreland Glass Company
Grapeville, Pennsylvania

This firm began as the Westmoreland Specialty Company in 1889. Glass articles intended for use as candy or mustard containers were very popular in this concern's early days. Pattern glass sets and oil lamps—typical products for many glass plants in the late nineteenth and early twentieth centuries—were also manufactured as was cut glass.

By 1920, the Westmoreland plant was a major force in the American tableware industry. The *National Glass Budget* reported that Westmoreland had the largest decorating facilities in the nation, and the decorated glassware shown in this book certainly reflects that strong interest. In the mid-1920s, the name of the organization was changed to Westmoreland Glass Company.

During the 1920s, Westmoreland made a great array of decorated glass, ranging from cutting, staining and etching to hand-painted enamel flowers and reverse painting as well as an original technique called "casing" which involved spraying with colored paint. Charles West obtained a design patent for a lattice-style decoration in 1924, and many Westmoreland items incorporated this motif.

Various opaque and transparent glass colors were made by Westmoreland during the 1920s and 30s. Among them are these: amber, amethyst, Aquamarine, Belgian blue, black, blue, canary yellow, green, Moonstone (opalescent), Roselin, ruby, topaz, and Wisteria.

The ownership of the company changed in 1937, and, as Charles West Wilson (grandson of Westmoreland's president) notes, the

firm's direction changed from the highly competitive arena of glass decorating to the manufacture of "reproductions" of 1880s-style glassware, mostly in milk glass. Westmoreland closed in 1984.

For more information on Westmoreland glass, see Lorraine Kovar's *Westmoreland Glass 1888-1940* (Marietta: Antique Publications, 1997) and Charles West Wilson's *Westmoreland Glass: Identification & Value Guide* (Paducah: Collector Books, 1996).

"Meet us in Pittsburgh in January" (Ft. Pitt Hotel)

Westmoreland Specialty Co.
Grapeville, Pa.

Manufacturers of High Grade Glassware—Plain, Cut and Decorated—for Gift Shops, Florists and Table Use.

No. 1707. Candy Jar. Made in ½-lb. and 1-lb. sizes. Fancy Decorations. Plain Colors and Gold Encrustations.

REPRESENTATIVES:

New York—H. C. Gray Co., 310 Fifth Avenue Bldg.
Philadelphia—Peacock & Roop, 1007 Filbert Street
Boston—H. P. & H. F. Hunt, 41 Pearl Street
San Francisco—Himmelstern Bros., 718 Mission Street
Dallas—D. D. Otstott, Inc., Southland Hotel Bldg.

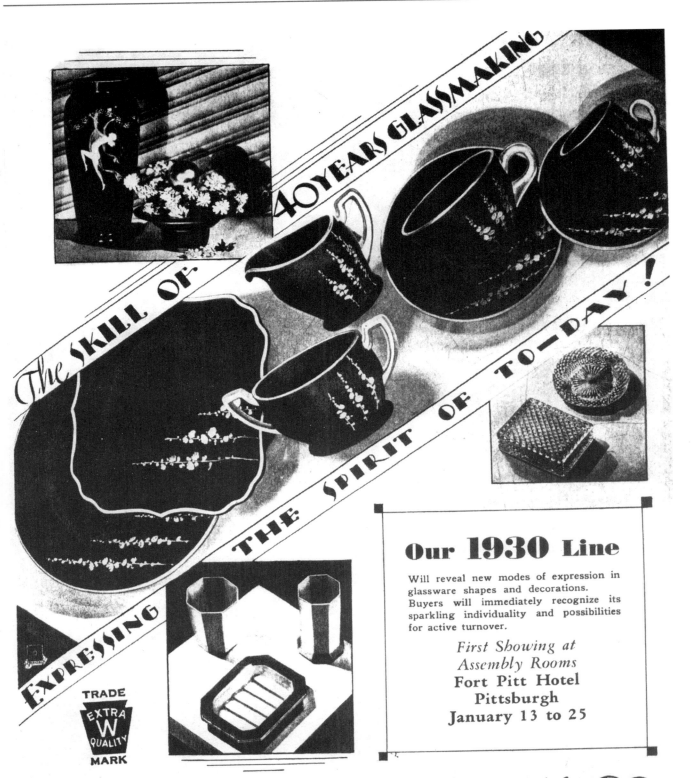

40 YEARS GLASSMAKING

THE SKILL OF

THE SPIRIT OF TO-DAY!

EXPRESSING

TRADE
EXTRA
W
QUALITY
MARK

Our **1930** Line

Will reveal new modes of expression in glassware shapes and decorations. Buyers will immediately recognize its sparkling individuality and possibilities for active turnover.

First Showing at Assembly Rooms
Fort Pitt Hotel Pittsburgh
January 13 to 25

WESTMORELAND GLASS CO., GRAPEVILLE PA.

MANUFACTURERS OF . . .
PLAIN-CUT AND DECORATED GLASSWARE FOR TABLE SERVICE-GIFT SHOPS-FLORISTS

Westmoreland
Glass Company
Grapeville, Pa.

Announcement

Our display during the 46th Annual Glass Exhibit as in former years, will be held in the

Assembly Rooms, Fort Pitt Hotel
Pittsburgh
From January 11th to 30th

A variety of beautiful new Shapes and new Designs in Colored, Decorated, Engraved, and Cut Glassware, also many attractive new shapes for Decorators and Cutters, will be shown.

We are also featuring reproductions of the old time Sandwich Glass which has again come into Vogue and these will be shown in high grade Crystal and beautiful shades of Amber, Green and Blue.

We cordially invite
you to visit us

WEST VIRGINIA GLASS SPECIALTY COMPANY
WESTON, WEST VIRGINIA

The last five pages of the color section in this book are drawn from a color catalogue issued by this company. Most of the items shown—pitcher/tumbler sets, punch sets, decanters and cocktail shaker sets—are beverage service items. Several more pages from this catalogue will be used in the next volume of this series.

The West Virginia Glass Specialty Company was one of several firms in Weston, West Virginia, which were under the control of Louie Wohinc, a former glassworker who became manager of the Weston Glass Company about 1919. Over a decade, Wohinc's empire grew to embrace the Louie Glass Company and the Weston Glass Company as well as the West Virginia Glass Specialty Company. The Louie enterprise was still in business in the 1990s, and, as Dean Six noted in an article in *Glass Collector's Digest* (December/January, 1994), the Wohinc-controlled firms produced remarkably similar products and colors at various times during the 1920s.

According to Six, Louie Wohinc assumed control of the Crescent Window Glass plant in 1929, converting it to a tableware operation and operating it under the West Virginia Glass Specialty Company name. The Weston Glass company was destroyed by fire in 1932, but the Louie Glass Company and the West Virginia Specialty ran in parallel until the West Virginia Specialty plant closed in 1987.

There is a good deal more to learn about all of these plants which operated in Weston during the 1920s and 1930s.

A NEW CREATION BY LOUIE

The West Virginia Glass Specialty Company, like other Louie units, has long been famous for its extensive and beautiful line of blown glassware, put out at a price that has staggered the trade. Heretofore these products have been mostly in the plain, though in both color and crystal.

But now a line of decorated ware is being shown which promises to create a new sensation. The tumbler and jug of the water set and the two items in stemware illustrated show merely one of the lovely decorations in platinum and matt finish. Many other items and many other treatments will shortly be available.

CALL AT NEW YORK OFFICE: 10 WEST 23rd STREET, NEW YORK

West Virginia Glass Specialty Company
LOUIE WOHINC, President

WESTON - - - WEST VIRGINIA

For 1937

A PREVIEW OF SOME OF OUR NEW ITEMS FOR THE COMING YEAR

The illustration shows our No. 741 Crimped Top Tropical Etched Vase; No. 105 Blue Bowl with Crystal Foot Vase, with band and line decoration No. 57; No. 455/455, 7 piece Refreshment Set including 10 oz. Jug partially frosted and adorned with band and line treatment No. 10. The last named is merely a variation of a type we have featured for some time but which has been so popular that we are showing it in a slightly different form for the new year. These are but a few of the many items and sets we will have (styled by Louie) to show the trade early in the year.

Our first display will be made at the Pittsburgh Glass and Pottery Show, William Penn Hotel, January 11-20. Be sure to see them. Also look for the new offerings by the Louie Glass Company.

WEST VIRGINIA GLASS SPECIALTY COMPANY

Louie Wohinc, President and General Manager.

WESTON,   **WEST VIRGINIA.**